Design for **Education**

Gensler

Gensler Publications
Two Harrison Street, Suite 400
San Francisco, CA 94105 USA

ISBN: 978-0-9826312-1-8

Library of Congress Control Number: 2010922394

Contents

Foreword

Look behind the prosperity of the world—not just its economic health, but also its cultural richness and social well-being—and you will find a robust education system. Even in the midst of a downturn, society invests in education to plant the seeds of a better future. Yet education institutions now face many of the same challenges and opportunities as other organizations. Campus buildings and their settings need to perform at a high level, both as evolving platforms for learning and as components of well-defined real-estate strategies. At the same time, they need to embody the qualities of place on which learning depends. To achieve this level of performance, our education clients increasingly look to other sectors for ideas and precedents. Gensler's diverse and global experience makes it a valued strategic advisor, recognizing that education is a unique endeavor and that every client has very specific needs.

Education institutions are typically long-lived. Even when they're brand new, they reflect a tradition that impels them to secure their future. This makes them the natural advocates of sustainability and stewardship. Their focus on learning makes them aware of how the design of the physical environment supports it. We believe that these traits make them ideal clients—knowledgeable, intellectually engaged, and highly collaborative. As architects and designers, we are interested in how buildings and settings enhance performance. Seeing our education clients as partners, we make their goals and strategies our starting point. The case studies in this book provide real-life examples of the issues, challenges, and opportunities these institutions face, and show how design—as a process of exploration and discovery—generates innovative and purposeful solutions. Drawn from our global education portfolio, they speak to the diversity of our education clients and our shared commitment to excellence.

M. Arthur Gensler Jr., FAIA, FIIDA, RIBA
Founder and Chairman, Gensler

Andrew P. Cohen, FAIA
David Gensler
Diane Hoskins, FAIA
Executive Directors, Gensler

OPPOSITE •• **The New Hall student residences at Notre Dame de Namur University in Belmont, California, feature shaded exterior walkways and staircases to foster interaction.**

Introduction by Andrew Blum

It might seem that a middle school outside London has little in common with an urban university in New York, a community college in Los Angeles, or a business school campus in Delhi—all of which are current or recent Gensler education projects. Yet amid the remarkably diverse body of work collected in this book, a defining thread emerges: the architecture is always in service to its institution.

Gensler's goal is never to employ a particular off-the-shelf solution, architectural form, or signature style, but rather to use the specific occasion that a building project affords to sharpen—and perhaps even recast—the longstanding purpose of a place. That was the refrain I heard over the course of my conversations with education practice leaders across Gensler: their eagerness to engage with the challenges facing institutions, and to do so as part of a relationship that continues to build over time.

Of course, Gensler's practice area leaders also see trends that affect the design of education settings. Most notably, the "talking head" style of lecturing is giving way to an interactive approach. Peer learning is increasingly important and supported. At universities and colleges, technology often makes lectures available 24/7, so the tutorial is a more important real-time destination than the lecture hall. From the student perspective, there's also a need for greater on-campus creature comforts—from student hubs that combine learning with social life to recreation of every sort, indoors and out.

New approaches to learning require new spaces to support them. Flexibility is crucial, which means "education space" is increasingly multiuse space, with classroom buildings giving way to hybrid settings that make fuller use of campus real estate, reducing the overall need for it. Sustainable design is a given now for education institutions, and there is a growing recognition that utilizing existing and new buildings and settings more effectively can also reduce the carbon footprint.

For Gensler, these trends and issues are starting points, not the defining characteristics of a specific institution or project. Education evolves today at a faster pace than in the past, reflecting a range of inputs—demographic, cultural, economic, and technological. As this suggests, education also changes markedly from place to place and among different types of institutions. What stands out is their remarkable singularity. Education clients never ask Gensler for "one of those." Design is invariably a conversation about ends and means. Equally, it's an exploration—how to realize education goals through the medium of a campus or a building and its settings. When a community college seeks to reorganize its curriculum around "green-collar" jobs, repurposing an old tire factory for a postindustrial economy is suddenly, strikingly relevant. That's the power of design in the service of goals and ideas.

Expecting the unexpected

Gensler approaches design in an interdisciplinary way, drawing consciously and systematically on its experience in different markets and regions. The firm's education practice reflects and benefits from a deep bench of experts in workplace design, hospitality, retail, sports and entertainment, and other sectors—and from the experience of working in many different regions and cultures. This breadth of knowledge serves as a springboard to innovation, often taking the design in unexpected directions.

This approach benefits education clients in several ways. First, many of their projects are essentially mixed use. When they look for relevant precedents, they often find them outside the campus. Second, they are looking for leverage—higher density of use, lower operating costs, and more effective support of people and programs. Like their counterparts in government, education clients are in it for the long haul. Sustainability in all its forms is a natural fit, because they will be around to reap its benefits. Flexibility is equally important—many institutions suffer from buildings that have become old before their time.

Another benefit of Gensler's breadth and depth is higher education's increasingly international thrust. With the BRIC countries—Brazil, Russia, India, and China—emerging as an economic force, Western institutions are establishing satellite programs and campuses in their cities. The expansion of Duke University's Fuqua School of Business in China and India is only one example. Gensler is arguably the leading design partner of global organizations. The firm's ability to work seamlessly across borders and cultures is a big advantage for universities as they move beyond their home campuses.

To be successful, Gensler believes, designers must themselves engage in the crucial process of learning. The understanding gained along the way is what spurs creativity toward a more apt solution. As a design community, Gensler is intrinsically curious. This curiosity is wide-ranging, considering the context of a project broadly in an effort to define what exactly is required of it. Gensler designers don't claim to have the answers, but instead are open to the ideas and insights that will lead to a successful outcome. As in the classroom, asking the right questions is often more important than "knowing the answers."

Learning is everywhere

Most education institutions today need to do more with less. They want their spaces to work harder. Doing so requires a careful alignment of architecture and pedagogy. It helps that this has been the crux of education's evolution over the last half-century, toward a broader range of learning environments. What used to be a hierarchical activity confined to lecture halls and classrooms has cracked wide open.

The consequences for the design of education settings are enormous. At Lone Star College–Cy-Fair outside Houston, the directive from the president was, "Every place you design must directly support learning." In planning a ground-up, 200-acre campus around the idea that learning is everywhere, Gensler understood that every last component of it had to do double or triple duty. By responding to learning's new ubiquity, the college supports the life of the community, which also uses the college's facilities. Because the buildings do more, there are fewer of them. The campus is compact and walkable, preserving open space for recreation and future growth. And as they walk, students can learn directly from a campus that works with nature to mitigate the summer heat and handle the Houston area's sometimes torrential rain.

Creating community

Lone Star College is not alone in reaching out to its community. Many schools and universities are now doing so, acknowledging their economic and other roles, finding new uses and users for their facilities, and providing students a range of amenities beyond what the school or campus can offer. Learning spaces are also becoming communication hubs, at both the institutional and urban scale. At Columbia College Chicago, Gensler was asked to increase the visibility of an urban campus spread across 22 different buildings in the Loop. There's no grassy quad here to lend identity, so Gensler began that process with a "corridors blitz." Completed over a summer, Gensler repainted the buildings' many hallways in a neutral palette and hung reproductions of student works to create a gallery-like ambience that speaks to the college's arts and design focus. Elevator lobbies were painted in bright colors. At very modest cost, the blitz made Columbia College's buildings visually consistent and easier to navigate. Architectural and graphic moves on the outsides of the buildings gave the college real presence in the Loop.

New York City's St. John's University opened the new D'Angelo Center at the end of 2009. At Gensler's urging, the building combined what were to be two separate projects, a classroom building and a university center, into what has quickly become both the gateway of the campus and its 24/7 social hub. St. John's, which attracts commuting as well as residential students, wanted both to feel part of a single community. Sited as close as possible to transit, D'Angelo Center shifts the center of gravity of the campus, acknowledging the ties it enjoys with the metropolis it has served since the 19th century.

The new imperative

Education institutions are returning to their roots. There's a sharper awareness of goals and purposes. Across the sector, leverage—getting the highest possible return on a carefully delimited investment—is a crucial success factor. This makes design a necessarily collaborative process, a partnership that puts the education client and the architect on the same team, weighing the same complex variables. All of the expectations are still there, but how to meet them demands, if anything, even greater creativity. The desire for sustainability, flexibility, and density of use reinforces this by combining an economy of means with an emphasis on results. Gensler is primed to thrive in this new environment because its ethos is so closely aligned with this kind of thinking.

It's no accident that Gensler is helping Kent County in the UK to transform its schools at every level, reorganizing them around a new concept for how these settings can support diverse learning styles effectively. Nor is it accidental that Gensler's education practice is involved with developer-led and design-build delivery, and is the partner of leading institutions as they seek higher-growth venues offshore for their world-renowned programs.

Learning is imperative. Education is crucial to economic development. The high-tech industry that began in Silicon Valley benefited from Stanford University's presence, while UC Berkeley and UC San Francisco have had similar roles in the rise of the biotech industry. Every industry cluster invariably has a regional network of schools, colleges, and universities behind it, providing its knowledge workforce and the scientific, technical, creative, and entrepreneurial talent to keep it growing. Gensler gets this connection, not least because of its longstanding global relationships with industry clusters.

These are not ordinary times. When new thinking is required, Gensler is the perennial change agent of choice. Freed from the ideology of style, these architects take the challenges of their education clients seriously. The work featured in this book exemplifies their range, responsiveness, and fluid creativity.

Andrew Blum, a correspondent for *Wired* and a contributing editor at *Urban Omnibus* and *Metropolis*, writes on architecture, urbanism, and technology. His writing has also appeared in the *New Yorker*, the *New York Times*, *Business Week*, and *Architectural Record*. He lives and works in New York.

Universities and colleges

Higher education's challenging context

The thread that ties together Gensler's diverse higher education practice is not the form the different buildings take, but how their design reflects the goals and strategies of each university or college.

In the world of higher education, every building project is both institutional *and* architectural. For Gensler, this means starting the conversation about the design earlier in the process, when the goals and strategies that will inform are first discussed. While clients know when they need architecture, the architecture they need has to reflect their institution's broader intentions if the building is to perform as designed. Every project has to be the occasion for new thinking, not just a response to a brief.

No wonder then that the challenging context of higher education is as discernible in these pages as the buildings themselves. Colleges and universities have enormous needs, and even greater constraints. New buildings require Herculean feats of budgeting, programming, and consensus. And a project must serve many masters—from students to trustees and even to the planet—over its full life cycle. In sum, all construction today has to be strategic. There are trends in higher education that constantly bring the same issues to the fore, yet they play out in ways that are unique to each and every institution.

Many of these projects began with a visioning process, a key means Gensler employs to surface both the strategic drivers and the cultural and institutional nuances that bring a program statement to life. Visioning engages the client in the collaborative process of design. Inviting the client to speak broadly about the project, the team listens and asks questions. Often, this is part of an ongoing dialogue with the institution as new projects extend the relationship and add to the design team's understanding.

While some higher education clients take an evolutionary approach to their buildings, others are eager for a dramatic break from their immediate past. Gensler's South Gate campus for East Los Angeles College is an example. The sustainability and renewable energy policies of Los Angeles Community College District required all new buildings constructed as part of a $6 billion modernization program to achieve LEED certification. That move represents a strategic investment in reducing the district's energy costs. Yet, like many projects today, it has other drivers. The focus on sustainability also addresses the goal of revamping the college's curriculum to prepare its students for "green-collar" jobs. South Gate epitomizes why so many

13

institutions are going green: the connection between education and environmental benefits. It's all part of a coming "harmonic convergence" as academic courses, the physical environment, and research all coalesce around the broad idea of sustainability.

It's a given that multiple factors are always in play. For the Richard C. Blum Center for Developing Economies at the University of California, Berkeley, the Gensler design team first functioned as strategic advisors, helping to fine-tune the program and financial aspects of the project early in the process, before design began in earnest. As always, flexibility was crucial. Believing *solution* to be a verb, not a noun, the team approached the Blum Center as a container of multiple activities that will inevitably change over time.

The Blum Center renovates and extends an existing landmark, the Naval Architecture Building. For the beloved older structure (built in 1914) to be reused, it had to join seamlessly with a new addition. Together, they also had to fit into a setting that is dominated by a larger new building nearby. Gensler's design skillfully arranges the Blum Center's different components to define the northwest corner of a new courtyard that serves the center and its neighbor, making them a real destination on the campus.

In some cases, an institution needs to fit in with broad and varied cultural contexts, as well as its own strategic needs. Duke University's Fuqua School of Business recently launched an expansion program, aimed at giving it a global presence. The first two global centers—in Kunshan, China, and Delhi, India— are meant to outwardly reflect the ideals of the school while being sympathetic to their physical and social environs. Gensler's designs incorporate robust sustainability programs and architecture that reflects both the International style and local traditions, as well as specific site considerations.

In other cases, the greater challenge is reflecting the distinct identities of individual units within a large and varied institution. For three projects at New York University (NYU), Gensler created state-of-the-art facilities within older buildings. These facilities illustrate how well the designers have balanced the specific needs of each program with the overall ethos of the university. The Wasserman Center for Career Development, for example, is one of NYU's "front doors" to the business community, providing state-of-the-art facilities for recruiting presentations and interviews. It's also a connecting point for career-minded alumni, and—with its café and wireless lounge—a popular student hangout.

Gensler's education architects have a particular interest in making buildings and spaces work harder. There's a fundamental willingness to challenge the limits that institutions set for themselves, and extend the realm of the possible. As one practice leader described it: "Design has the ability to make 1+1=3. That may not be good math, but it definitely adds up for our university and college clients."

OPPOSITE •• **At The George Washington University in Washington, DC, the redesigned 5,000-seat arena allows the action to take center stage, with enhanced seating, lighting, and signage.**

University of the Pacific

Don and Karen DeRosa University Center
Stockton, California, USA

In brief

Type: Campus center
Completed: 2008
Size: 55,000 sf
Height: 2 stories
LEED NC Silver

Founded in 1851, the University of the Pacific has been in Stockton since 1925. Many of the older classroom and residential buildings on the campus are in the academic style of that era, with gabled roofs and brick façades. Pacific asked Gensler to create a "third place" that could serve as a social destination for the community. The university center's location is pivotal, linking the academic core to student housing across the Calaveras River. Accessible to both, it houses a rich and inviting mix of activities, including live music performance. Daylight is an important design element—and the building is LEED Silver certified.

OPPOSITE •• The Lair is an informal place for hanging out with friends, studying, listening to live music, hitting the game room for some interactive excitement, or drifting to an alcove for conversation. The exposed gable roof structure is washed in ambient daylight from the roof ridge lights and clerestory windows. OVERLEAF •• The center's entry plaza and main lobby, flanked by the two smaller pavilions. Differences in their placement and roof treatment give the pavilions a subtle asymmetry.

Don and Karen DeRosa
University Center

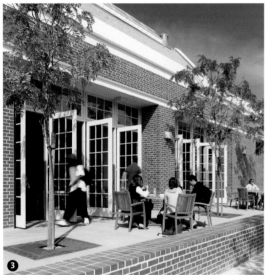

The University of the Pacific's Stockton campus houses the undergraduate programs that attract students from around the world. To retain them, the university provides a traditional academic setting with a variety of student housing and an array of activities to support a full on-campus social life. Music is especially important—the university counts jazz great Dave Brubeck as an alumnus. Developed over time on land north and south of the Calaveras River, the campus lacked a central gathering place. The DeRosa University Center occupies a pivotal location just south of the river. Gensler designed it to pull the campus together and make it much more accessible from the rest of the campus.

The center's gabled roofs and brick façades acknowledge the campus's past. Its linear plan reflects widespread local practice in California's Central Valley, limiting east-west exposures and allowing cross-ventilation. The plan organizes the center's different activities around an interior promenade. On the lower level, they include a bookstore, the Marketplace servery, the Pacific Commons dining hall, and a conference center with an event hall. These spaces open to outdoor settings used for everything from large receptions to informal barbecues. Upstairs are the River Room, a formal dining room; meeting rooms; the Brickyard, a casual dining and gathering space; the Lair pub; Student Life offices; and two outdoor decks. Gensler reduced the apparent mass by housing the program in three pavilions, the larger one facing the river and the two smaller ones facing the academic core. The strategy relates the building to its older neighbors and defines a built edge along the river—given porosity by the portals, terraces, and through-building views along that façade.

The center is a modern, high-performance building with a range of sustainable features. Natural light is an integral feature of the interior, designed using Lawrence Berkeley National Laboratory's Radiance software to validate the lighting levels. Sun shading and trellises shelter the outdoor terraces from the summer heat. The gable roofs' operable ridge lights combine with clerestory windows and operable doors and transoms to provide convection cooling. Low velocity air, sent through under-floor and sidewall diffusers, reduces energy use and improves indoor air quality. Sensors turn on the building's powered systems only when they're needed. Low-flow plumbing fixtures are used throughout, cutting water use by half, and, the center's lighting power consumption is 45 percent lower than required by California's Title 24 energy code. Bio-swales treat roof and site runoff. As it extends toward the river, the new landscape around the center melds with the riparian setting.

Green facts

Daylight sensors reduce light power by	Low-flow fixtures cut water use by
45%	**48**%

OPPOSITE ••

1: The promenade, viewed from the northeast, with the Pacific Commons dining hall visible below.
2: Each pavilion relates in scale and appearance to the traditional buildings elsewhere on campus.
3: The center supports an indoor-outdoor lifestyle in a way that allows for cross-ventilation.
4: Both the dining hall and conference center are served from the Marketplace kitchen/servery.
5: The River Room provides faculty, staff, and students with a formal dining area with river views.
6: Outdoor terraces tie the building to the larger campus, with great views of its varied landscape.

Site plan 0   100   200   400 ft

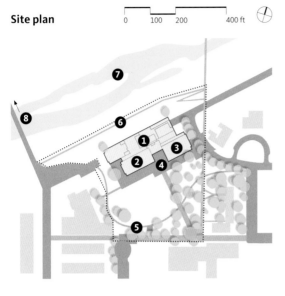

BELOW •• The light-filled main lobby, off the entry plaza, provides access to activities on the promenade and upper level. It can double as a large indoor gathering space, with the stairway serving as a stage. OPPOSITE •• The outdoor terrace at the southwest corner of the building is a popular place to congregate. PAGE 24 •• View of the promenade from the northwest, with the Pacific Commons dining hall below.

1: North pavilion
2: Southwest pavilion
3: Southeast pavilion
4: Entry plaza

5: Meandering path
6: Riverfront walk
7: Calaveras River
8: Pedestrian bridge

23

Lower-level floor plan

1: Bookstore
2: Marketplace servery
3: Kitchen
4: Promenade
5: Fire pit terrace
6: Entrance lobby
7: Pacific Commons dining hall
8: Event hall

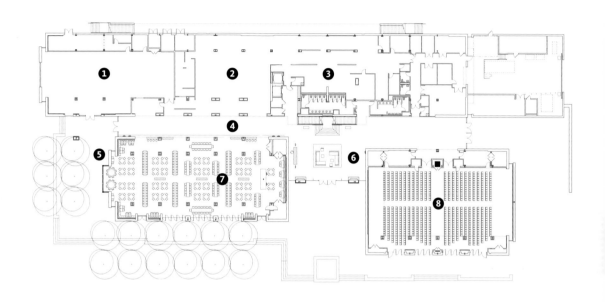

Upper-level floor plan

1: West deck
2: East deck
3: Student Life offices
4: The Lair (pub)
5: The Brickyard
6: Conference center
7: The River Room

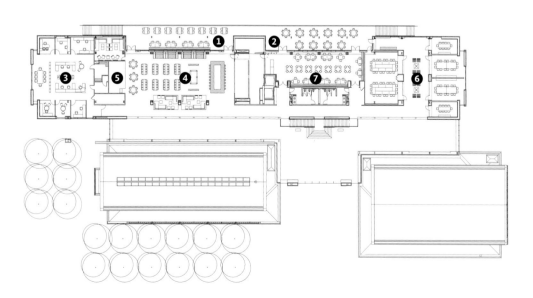

BELOW •• The LEED Silver-certified building integrates a variety of sustainable measures, both inside and outside the building, as shown in these two sectional diagrams.

1: Bio-swales mitigate roof and site runoff
2: Roof shingles are of recycled rubber
3: Roof trusses use FSC-certified wood
4: Low-flow fixtures cut water use by 48 percent
5: Low-velocity displacement diffusers reduce energy use and improve indoor air quality
6: Exterior cladding uses regionally sourced brick
7: Riparian landscape is protected along the riverfront
8: Operable doors and transoms allow ventilation and night cooling
9: Operable ridge lights bring in daylight and allow stack ventilation
10: Daylight sensors adjust lighting to save power
11: Under-floor air is provided in Student Life offices
12: Clerestory windows provide ambient daylight
13: Integral sun-shading protects decks and terraces

OPPOSITE, TOP •• View of the building from the south. Its location and north- and south-facing entries tie it to other parts of the campus, shifting the community's center of gravity. OPPOSITE, BOTTOM •• The Brickyard is a popular place to congregate on the upper level, overlooking the river. Activity areas are fitted into alcoves around the larger space.

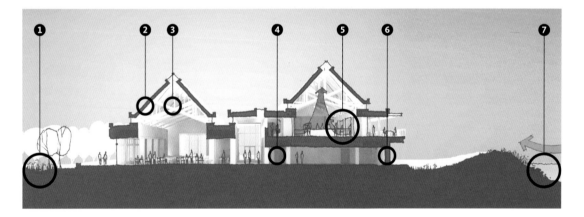

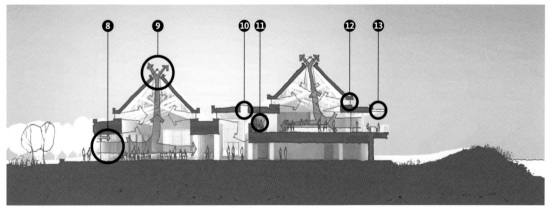

27

Notre Dame de Namur University

New Hall and Campus Master Plan
Belmont, California, USA

In brief

Type: Residence hall
Completed: 2005
Size: 41,329 sf
Height: 3 stories
Green factor: Sustainably designed

Seventeen years after its formation, the College of Notre Dame became the first women's college in California chartered to grant the baccalaureate degree in 1868. In 1922, the college purchased the summer home of Bank of California founder William Ralston—a wooded, 50-acre estate in Belmont, south of San Francisco. In 2001, Gensler completed a new master plan and design guidelines for the campus that coincided with its becoming Notre Dame de Namur University. New Hall is part of a new cluster of academic, residential, and community buildings that will densify and activate the campus at its core, while preserving its wooded, park-like character. Along with the new student housing, Gensler designed the planned Campus Center nearby— as the locus of student social life at the university.

OPPOSITE •• A glazed "sky lounge" directly above the archway into New Hall's courtyard gives passersby a sense of the activity within the residences. With its wood cladding and long, low-rise form, New Hall fits into the existing landscape. **ABOVE** •• Operable windows and narrow floor plates facilitate natural ventilation. Shading structures reduce solar heat gain. Generously sized staircases foster chance meetings and conversations.

By the late 1990s, the College of Notre Dame was planning its transition to a university. The campus demographics had changed—35 percent of its student body was nonresidential, commuting to the campus by car. Meeting their needs meant new buildings and infrastructure—and pushing enrollment beyond a 1,500-student cap agreed to with Belmont. Gensler's new campus plan, completed in parallel with the reorganization of the college as Notre Dame de Namur University, uses an innovative infill development strategy to minimize the impact of future growth. New buildings are concentrated at the center of the campus, leaving much of the periphery as the wooded park valued by town and gown alike. The plan reflects the shared vision of the university and the Belmont community, creating a memorable, visually cohesive setting that preserves campus identity and sensitively and sustainably allows new growth.

New Hall is the opening move in a new cluster of buildings and outdoor settings at the heart of the campus. Completed in 2005, the three-story, wood-clad complex houses 200 students in three- and four-bedroom suite configurations. New Hall is located along the outer edge of the cluster, bordering the campus nature preserve, as its informal character—angling around a bluff—reflects. Configured as two long bars, the residence hall has narrow floor plates to capture daylight and afternoon breezes for cross-ventilation in every suite. Shaded exterior circulation enhances a sense of community and the opportunities for interaction. New Hall includes a resident director apartment, staff offices, a lounge, and a laundry room. Students have their own rooms, sharing the living room and bathroom with their suitemates.

Site plan   0   16   32   64 ft

1: Typical unit
2: Entry (lounge above)
3: Resident director apartment
4: New Hall office
5: Landscaped courtyard
6: Laundry unit
7: Mechanical/ electrical

OPPOSITE •• Exterior circulation on both sides of an outdoor plaza creates plenty of opportunities for students to run into each other and strengthen bonds, building community. **OVERLEAF** •• Trees, trellises, and overhangs shade the walkways and landscaped plaza to encourage socializing.

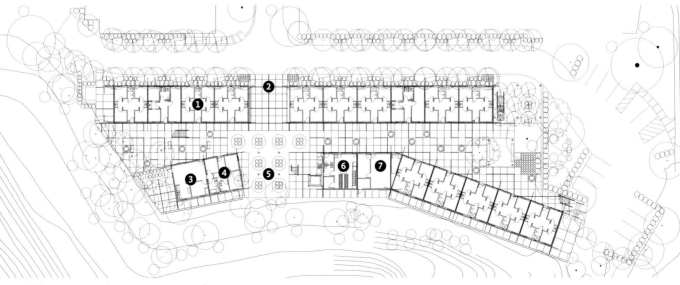

30

BELOW •• The master plan restores the campus to a more pastoral collegiate environment, keeping cars and parking areas away from central areas to coax students to walk or bike instead.

OPPOSITE •• Designed to pair with New Hall, the Campus Center building will serve as the university's social heart. It houses a dining hall, a bookstore, event spaces, and student program rooms.

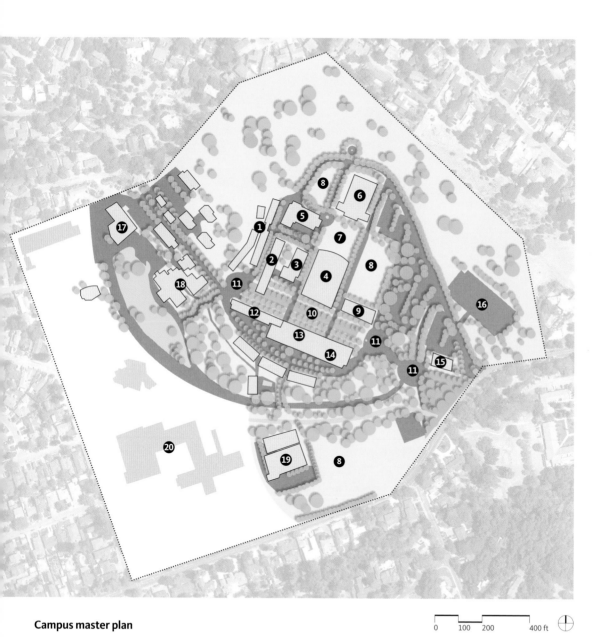

Campus master plan

0   100   200   400 ft

1: New Hall
2: St. Joseph's Hall
3: Campus Center
4: Library
5: Cunningham Chapel

6: Gymnasium
7: Spiritual Garden
8: Recreation field
9: Residence hall
10: Great lawn

11: Plaza
12: Julie Billiart Hall
13: Academic Building
14: St. Mary's Hall
15: Taube Center

16: Parking structure
17: Art center & gallery
18: Ralston Hall
19: Theater
20: High School

University of California, Berkeley

**The Richard C. Blum Center for
Developing Economies
Berkeley, California, USA**

In brief

Type: Research center
Completion: 2010
Size: 22,000 sf
Height: 3 stories
LEED NC registered, targeting Silver

UC Berkeley, the original campus of the University of California, is one of the world's leading public research universities. The College of Engineering is at the heart of that global reputation, part of the intellectual capital that has made the Bay Area a powerhouse of innovation. The Richard C. Blum Center for Developing Economies brings together multidisciplinary teams to develop solutions to alleviate global poverty. Located in the campus's engineering quadrant, the Blum Center complex renovates and expands a national historic landmark, John Galen Howard's 1914 Naval Architecture Building, to provide a light-filled, three-story space shared by the center and the college.

ABOVE ●● Former Vice President Al Gore and UC Regent Richard Blum toss the first shovelfuls of dirt at the groundbreaking ceremony for the Blum Center. OPPOSITE ●● The new wing, modern but compatible with the Naval Architecture Building, is placed at a 16-foot distance, respecting the historic structure's integrity.

OPPOSITE, TOP •• Perimeter glazing below the new wing's roof brings daylight to the top floor. **OPPOSITE, BOTTOM** •• Extensive use of glass illuminates the Blum Foundation entry at the podium level, while providing views of the outdoor plaza and the campus. **OVERLEAF** •• The podium, first-level terrace, and open bridge link the historic building and new wing, framing a landscaped plaza that provides the entire College of Engineering with places to socialize, collaborate, and reflect.

Site plan

1: Blum Center
2: Naval Arch. Bldg.
3: North Gate Hall
4: Hearst Avenue
5: Sutardja Dai Hall
6: Davis Hall
7: Hesse Hall
8: Haviland Road
9: Etcheverry Hall
10: Soda Hall

The University of California's Berkeley campus, the institution's oldest and largest, began operations in 1869. The 178-acre main campus occupies a park-like, hillside site overlooking the San Francisco Bay. Between 1903 and 1924, John Galen Howard, supervising architect for the first campus plan, designed 20 Beaux-Arts buildings that form the core of the campus. He also designed several shingle-style structures that are now campus landmarks, including the Naval Architecture Building.

On April 23, 2009, Nobel laureate Al Gore joined financier, philanthropist, and University of California regent Richard C. Blum for the groundbreaking of the future home of the Blum Center for Developing Economies. In his remarks, the former US Vice President predicted that the building "will quickly become a center of global importance." The hugely popular interdisciplinary program connects UC Berkeley's engineering, scientific, and design talent to counterparts in developing countries, the *San Francisco Chronicle* reported. The Blum Center's goal is to develop affordable solutions to such endemic problems of impoverished communities as the lack of clean drinking water, adequate sanitation, and reliable energy sources.

To give the Blum Center suitable quarters, Gensler is renovating and expanding the Naval Architecture Building. The renovation will bring the existing structure up to current seismic, life safety, and accessibility standards, and connect it visually and functionally to a new wing that more than doubles the square footage. Responding to its historic counterpart with a modern interpretation, the new wing has a wood and glass skin and a pitched roof, which floats above the wood rain-screen wall to allow natural light to filter deep into the top floor. The existing and new structures share a ground floor and terrace, with an open bridge connecting them at the second floor. The ground floor provides space for student/faculty collaboration. The Blum Center, along with nearby Sutardja Dai Hall, defines a new landscaped plaza for the College of Engineering. The project is being designed to achieve LEED Silver.

BELOW •• Appropriate for an interdisciplinary program focused on addressing pressing issues of reliable energy sources and clean drinking water, the Blum Center incorporates a number of sustainable design strategies, outlined in the diagram below, to reduce its energy and water use.

1: The roof overhangs and sunshades reduce solar heat gain during the summer months
2: Glazing beneath the roof captures daylight and heat during the winter months
3: Operable windows draw in cooling breezes and exhaust heat from the interior
4: The thermal mass of the concrete helps moderate temperatures within the new wing
5: The 15-foot floor-to-floor heights and sloped roof let heat rise, keeping occupants cool
6: FSC-certified cedar shingles on the new wing come from sustainably managed forests

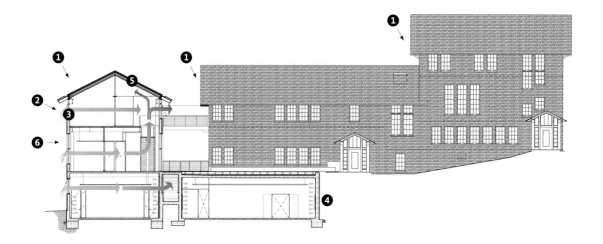

Green facts

Existing structure and envelope retained

75%

FSC-certified wood finishes/materials

50%

Reduced water use for irrigation

50%

Recycled/salvaged construction waste

50%

OPPOSITE •• The design team used a three-dimensional model to study the Blum Center's addition's relation to the Naval Architecture Building, Sutardja Dai Hall, and their shared plaza, a gathering place that is part of a cross-campus walkway on axis with UC Berkeley's Campanile.

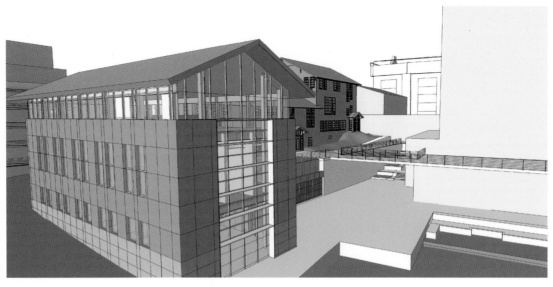

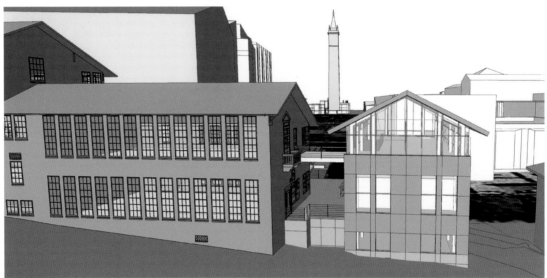

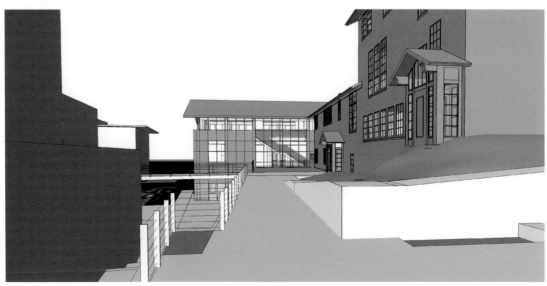

New York University

**The Wasserman Center for Career Development
and Steinhardt School James L. Dolan Recording/
Teaching Complex and Department of
Speech-Language Pathology and Audiology
New York, New York, USA**

In brief

Type: Urban campus renovation
Completed: 2006–2009
Size: 7,500–20,000 sf
Green factor: Adaptive reuse

With 50,000 students, New York University (NYU) is America's largest private university. It is also an urban campus, with its academic buildings clustered in and around Washington Square in Manhattan. Gensler has partnered with NYU on multiple projects, including the Wasserman Center, serving NYU students and alumni; and two for departments of NYU's Steinhardt School of Culture, Education, and Human Development. These projects created state-of-the-art facilities in existing, often older, buildings. Two of them integrate advanced technology and stringent acoustical requirements. Given Manhattan's urbane, entrepreneurial culture, the designs are rigorous in both a professional and an academic sense that speaks to NYU's importance to a city that competes internationally for talent.

OPPOSITE •• **A diagonal block of reception, support, and office spaces—clad from floor to ceiling in dark bamboo—serves as the central organizing element of the Wasserman Center.**

Campus plan

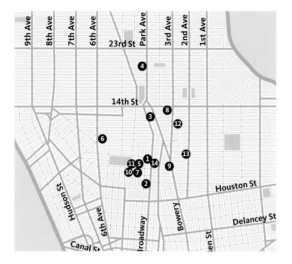

1: 726–730 Broadway
2: 665 Broadway
3: 838 Broadway
4: 250 Park Avenue South
5: 14 Washington Place
6: 58 W. 10th Street/Creative Writers House
7: 40 W. 4th Street

8: 133 E. 13th Street
9: 20 Cooper Square
10: 70 Washington Square South/Bobst Library
11: 35 W. 4th Street
12: 75 3rd Avenue
13: 113 2nd Avenue
14: 715–721 Broadway

The Wasserman Center for Career Development
133 East 13th Street

The Wasserman Center for Career Development consolidates a range of career-related services on the mezzanine level of Palladium Hall, an NYU residential building near Union Square. The vision, according to Trudy Steinfeld, the center's executive director, was to combine "the feel of a professional office environment with the energy of a thriving student center or downtown design firm." The existing mezzanine was low and dark. Gensler opened it up by exposing the ceiling, brightening the walls, and using glass walls and doors to bring daylight into the interior. With a café and wireless lounges, Wasserman Center is a popular student and alumni destination. The space is organized around a central "bamboo block"—a bamboo-clad bar of office/support space set alongside a diagonal circulation path that leads from reception to support areas that, in Steinfeld's words, "are the envy of Fortune 500 employers." They include a large area for presentations, as well as centers for student and alumni career counseling and development, and for employers and interviewing. The design offsets denser areas for one-to-one conversation with open areas for mixing and discussion.

OPPOSITE •• At the Wasserman Center, students can tap into information on potential employers and find career opportunities in the Career Resource Room.

James L. Dolan Recording/Teaching Complex
35 West 4th Street

Gensler collaborated with Steinhardt School Department of Music and Performing Arts Professions faculty and recording studio/acoustical specialist Walters-Storyk to design the 7,500-square-foot Dolan Recording/Teaching Complex. The view from the reception area into the cutting-edge control room immediately establishes the department as an advanced teaching facility. The complex occupies the entire sixth floor of an early-20th-century building off Washington Square. The challenge was to fit an extremely dense program into a relatively tight space, giving students sufficient work areas and visual access to instructors. As a complicating factor, four floor-to-ceiling steel trusses slice through the space. The control room and other critical sound isolation areas are fitted within them without compromising their ease of access or functionality. A raised floor ensures future flexibility. The Dolan complex includes a 25-seat control/classroom, a live room large enough for musical ensembles, and several research labs, including one for three-dimensional audio experimentation. The transparency of the space makes the recording process visible and brings in daylight.

OPPOSITE, TOP •• One look at the cutting-edge control room confirms the Department of Music and Performing Arts Professions' strong reputation. **OPPOSITE, BOTTOM ••** Quintets and other ensembles can be comfortably accommodated in the recording studio. **BELOW, LEFT ••** The recording suite—studio and control room—are skillfully fitted into a relatively compact space. **BELOW, RIGHT ••** The wayfinding and signage are designed with a playful twist. **OVERLEAF ••** The 25-seat control room/classroom gives students direct experience with the complexities of audio recording and direction.

Department of Speech-Language Pathology and Audiology
665 Broadway

Needing larger quarters, the Steinhardt School's Department of Speech-Language Pathology and Audiology asked Gensler to renovate a full floor of a 19th-century building. The new facility addresses the related needs of faculty and administrators, student clinicians, and patients. The speech-language hearing clinic, staffed by faculty and students, uses audiovisual techniques in diagnosis and therapy. The technology is seamlessly integrated, with visual cues guiding people through the space, giving it flexibility for change and growth. The design enhances the user experience by giving the reception and study areas natural light, and by providing details that appeal to patients of all ages. Entries to the clinic observation room have sculptural panels that evoke sound waves, for example, while the audiology observation–testing room is decorated with red-and-white graphic wave patterns. Its deep-red felt panels are meant to be touched. The facility was recognized for outstanding design by *American School & University* magazine in 2008.

OPPOSITE •• The reception area, a bright space overlooking Lower Broadway, is designed to accommodate patients ranging from toddlers on up.

Floor plan

1: Clinic rooms
2: Faculty/clinician administration offices
3: Student study/pantry
4: Conference room
5: Audiology booth
6: Observation room
7: Lab/education
8: Faculty research space
9: Reception/waiting area

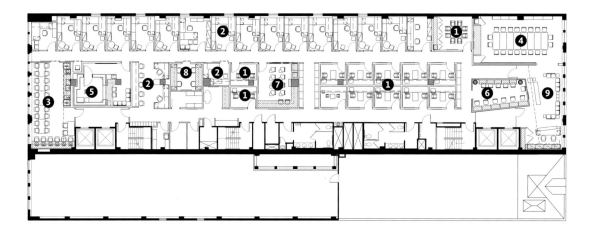

53

Columbia College Chicago

Campus Modernization
Chicago, IL, USA

In brief

Type: Urban campus renovation
Completion: 2005–ongoing
Size: 4,000–100,000 sf
Buildings to date: 15
Up to LEED CI Silver

From modest beginnings as a school of oratory, Columbia College Chicago has grown to have more than 12,000 undergraduate and graduate students. Its urban campus includes 23 buildings—2.5 million square feet—spread across Chicago's South Loop neighborhood. Actively engaged with the city's life and culture, the college wanted to strengthen the campus's physical connections with the downtown and create a sense of identity. Gensler responded with a series of strategic renovations of classrooms, workspaces, and common areas—using a shared design language. With true economy of means, these interventions have made the college much more visible, reinforcing its arts and media focus. They have enabled it to take full advantage of the urban setting, with buildings that are visually cohesive and easy to navigate.

OPPOSITE, TOP •• Gensler leveraged the Journalism Department's location in Chicago's South Loop to showcase the college to commuters on the city's elevated trains. OPPOSITE, BOTTOM •• Concurrent with Gensler's work on the inside of the buildings, the college launched a program to promote its identity on the outside. OVERLEAF, LEFT •• Outfitted to professional standards, the bustling newsroom is designed to support the fast pace of reporting and a changing array of reporters. OVERLEAF, RIGHT •• Corridors and other circulation spaces across the urban campus are designed as student gathering spaces.

As the South Loop neighborhood gentrified, the college wanted to create a hip, modern campus identity that communicated the school's focus on the arts and media and made the disparate buildings—built largely in the late 19th and early 20th centuries—function as coherent, supportive environments for faculty, staff, and students. Most interventions involved basic materials and details, with signature elements applied strategically in key areas. The first project, dubbed the "corridors blitz," recast the buildings' corridors as gallery-like settings enlivened by several hundred reproductions of student artwork. To make navigating the college's urban campus easier, each building was given its own bold color, large swaths of which mark elevator lobbies and stair lobbies.

Renovations also focused on creating places for gathering and interacting. At 600 South Michigan, the eighth floor became a multiuse "hoteling" office space where part-time faculty could meet peers and work between classes. The second floor of 33 East Congress Parkway, renovated for the Journalism Department, puts the production studio at the building's heart to serve as a unifying element; wrapped in corrugated metal, it houses a video production set and mixing lab. Five adjoining classrooms at 623 South Wabash had computers intended for student use, but it was hard to know if they were in use or not. Taking down walls to create a new area combining teaching and lab spaces—each defined visually by such features as carpeting and higher or lower ceilings—has increased computer use. One paid monitor can now oversee all 184 computers. Gensler also renovated the building's lobby, removing fake drywall arches and columns, exposing historic columns with plaster capitals, and adding generous seating areas to give students views onto the street—and making the college visible to passersby in the South Loop.

Other moves give the college greater public visibility on the exterior. The word *Columbia*, spelled out in bold letters across the Journalism Department's windows, greets the elevated trains that pass close by. At Anchor Graphics, a not-for-profit fine-art print shop affiliated with the college, sheer fabric curtains patterned with reflective sequins proved an inexpensive way to shield large second-floor windows from the heat of the sun, while letting in plenty of daylight and giving the shop a distinctive street presence. For the student residences at 731 South Plymouth Court, a new gathering place in the first-floor lobby offers not only pool and foosball tables, but also an informal performance stage area just inside the large street-facing windows. On the ground floor of 600 South Michigan, former maintenance space converted into an admissions tour center features 20-foot-wide, floor-to-ceiling windows, which give visiting prospective students first-hand views of the college's dynamic urban environment.

OPPOSITE •• **Acoustical "clouds" dampen the noise as they light the Learning Center. Movable walls provide privacy for tutoring.**

Green fact

Green measures: energy-efficient HVAC, low-flow fixtures, and environmentally safe paint with low-volatility organic compounds.

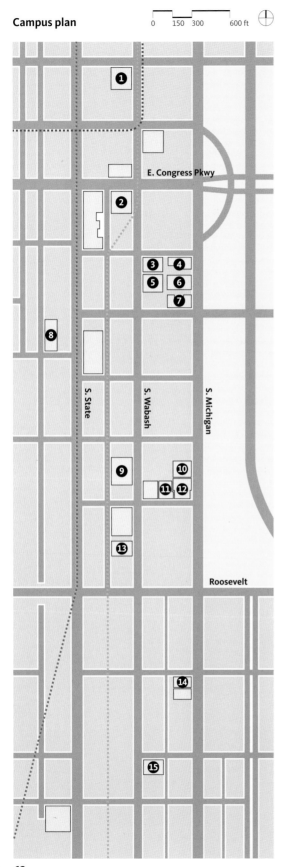

Campus plan

0 150 300 600 ft

E. Congress Pkwy

S. State

S. Wabash

S. Michigan

Roosevelt

LEFT ••

Located in Chicago's South Loop, Columbia College occupies 23 buildings that comprise 2.5 million square feet of space. Gensler has designed over 125 projects in 15 of the 23 buildings for the college, whose campus is a unique blend of industrial and mercantile buildings threaded together by the surrounding city streets.

1:	218 S. Wabash	9:	916 S. Wabash
2:	33 E. Congress Pkwy.	10: 1006 S. Michigan
3:	619 S. Wabash	11: 72 E. 11th Street
4:	600 S. Michigan	12: 1014 S. Michigan
5:	623 S. Wabash	13: 1112 S. Wabash
6:	618 S. Michigan	14: 1306 S. Michigan
7:	624 S. Michigan	15: 1415 S. Wabash
8:	731 S. Plymouth Ct.	

OPPOSITE ••

a: Quotes from famous journalists add interest to the corridor leading to the Journalism Department's faculty offices.

b: Open work settings in the Office of Campus Environment promote collaboration and the free flow of ideas.

c: Gensler converted a dark basement into the computer commons, a flexible workspace with a translucent ceiling and up-lit walls.

d: The Learning Center lobby is punctuated by a dynamic curving stair.

OVERLEAF •• At 618 South Michigan, the college capitalizes on its prominent location to highlight the work of its talented fashion design students and give the public a glimpse of college life.

623 South Wabash, 9th-floor plan

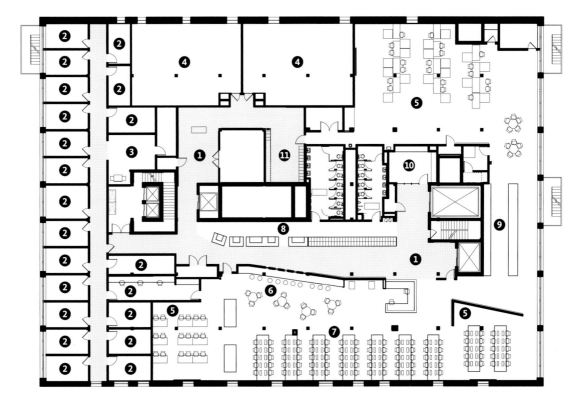

1: Circulation
2: Faculty offices
3: Pantry work room
4: Graphic arts computer lab
5: Open classroom
6: Laptop station
7: Open lab
8: Pin-up space
9: Layout area
10: Resource room
11: Lockers

OPPOSITE, TOP •• The renovated print shop's studio is designed to support the art and craft of printing and provide lots of wall space to display examples of student work. OPPOSITE, BOTTOM •• The street-level welcome center, a branded space with playful lighting and furniture, sets the tone for a college focused on arts and media. RIGHT •• Gensler combined five classrooms at 623 South Wabash to create an open computer lab that gets high use with minimal oversight.

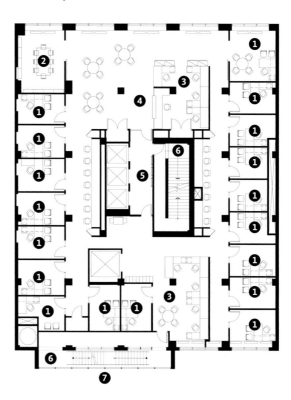

8th-floor plan

BELOW AND OPPOSITE •• **618 South Michigan**
In renovating the former Spertus Institute building on South Michigan, Gensler removed an exterior fire escape and replaced it with a cantilevered exit stairway. The new stairway is enclosed by a translucent wall that enlivens the back of the building, creating a glowing lantern visible from nearby college buildings.

1: Offices
2: Conference room
3: Open offices
4: Reception
5: Elevator lobby
6: Stairwell
7: Translucent glass wall

Duke University

Duke Global Campus
Kunshan, China
Fuqua School of Business Global Center
Delhi, India

In brief

Type: New campus (CN)/Academic complex (IN)
Completion (estimated): 2011/2012
Size: 201 acres/7.4 acres
Height: 2–4 stories
Green factor: Regionally responsive

Duke University's Fuqua School of Business ranks as one of America's top business schools. Now Fuqua has embarked on an expansion program aimed at making it the first truly global business school, establishing campuses in key economic and cultural centers around the world. As part of this effort, Gensler has planned a new Duke Global Campus in Kunshan, near Suzhou, just north of Shanghai, and is designing a six-building complex for Fuqua as its first phase. A second project under way is Fuqua's India Global Center in Delhi. Both projects are designed to support a wide range of learning styles and, emphasizing collaboration, incorporate business-class hospitality.

OPPOSITE, TOP •• At the new Kunshan campus, the Fuqua School of Business building's glass curtain wall and skylights fill the interior with daylight. **OPPOSITE, BOTTOM ••** Curved pavilion roofs recall traditional Chinese architecture.

ABOVE •• **The proposed master plan for the Kunshan campus preserves some 60% of the site as green space and incorporates water throughout.**

Duke Global Campus, Kunshan, China

Gensler planned Duke's Kunshan campus as a model of sustainable development, reflective of the natural and cultural context of the Suzhou region. The 201-acre site has a high water table, so 40 acres are left as undisturbed wetlands. About 4.55 million square feet of new academic, residential, conference, and service buildings will be developed, but some 60 percent of the site will be kept as green space that also incorporates manmade and natural lakes and canals. The campus draws on the region's traditional building practices as well as on modern precedents, with development that is sympathetic to the context, but contemporary in appearance and performance. The campus's use of daylight, solar shading, passive cooling, and natural flood control benefits from centuries of experience dealing with the opportunities and challenges of Kunshan's climate and terrain.

The first phase of the campus is the Gensler-designed Fuqua School of Business complex. It consists of five buildings, organized around a manmade lake and connected by bridges. The school's teaching programs are housed in the three-story building containing four tiered classrooms, an auditorium, a library, a dining room for students and conference participants, and a business center. A full-height central atrium serves as a campus gathering place, emblematic of the school's emphasis on collaboration and community. The atrium and roof terraces enjoy views of the lake to the west and the campus main quadrangle to the east.

The range of settings provided across the complex speaks to the diversity of learning styles that the school intends to support. Other phase one campus buildings include a four-story conference center, with 203 guest rooms and 20 suites, and a three-story academic incubator building, equipped with wet and dry labs, to allow Duke's academic programs at the campus to acclimatize before their full launch. Housing includes a two-story, 20-unit faculty residence with four live/work lofts; and a three-story, 200-bed student residence with suites that emulate the Unité model of Le Corbusier—each suite is entered from the second floor, with shared living on that level and four bedrooms (all singles) and two shared bathrooms above or below.

Proposed campus master plan

1: Fuqua School of
   Business
2: Conference center
3: Incubator building

4: Faculty residence
5: Student housing
6: Service buildings
7: Library

8: Student center
9: Cultural center
10: Athletics
11: Landmark buildings

0   50   100   200 ft

1: The Fuqua School of Business complex's business school, conference center, academic incubator building, and faculty and student residences surround a manmade lake.
2: A pedestrian bridge crossing the lake links the business school to the conference center.
3: The three-story student residence anchors the southwest corner of the campus.
4: The faculty residence, like other buildings in the business school complex, supports planted roofs and expansive glazing for natural light.

Green facts

Campus total open space

69%

Business school open space

45%

Performance facts

Total campus development capacity

4.55 m sf

Design fact

Site area of Fuqua School of Business complex

36.3 acres

Number of campus development phases

4

Number of campus car parking spaces

829

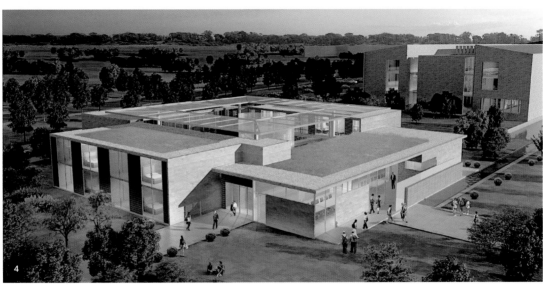

Site plan

1: School of Business
2: Conference center
3: Fitness center
4: Atrium/living rooms
5: Lounge
6: Dining
7: School store
8: Terrace
9: Guest room
10: Team rooms
11: Classrooms
12: Auditorium
13: Library/business center
14: Lake

0 25 50 100 ft

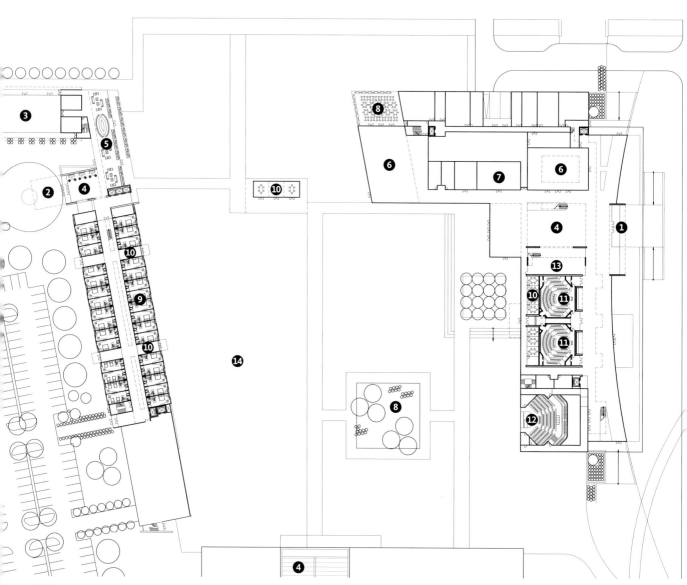

ABOVE •• **View of the lounge/reception area for the Fuqua School of Business Global Center in Delhi, India.**

Fuqua School of Business Global Center, Delhi, India

Fuqua's Global Center in Delhi will occupy a 7.4-acre undeveloped site on the outskirts of Delhi. Because of its peripheral location, the center would be prone to interruptions in key utility services, so the sustainable strategies Gensler has used in its planning and design emphasize a degree of self-sufficiency—onsite wastewater treatment, for example—in addition to reducing energy and water use, ensuring indoor air quality, and minimizing pollution and waste in construction and operation.

Gensler's design merges contemporary architecture with local and regional influences: the low-rise cast-in-place reinforced concrete structure has a modern glass-and-aluminum curtain wall system, while the layout, building orientations, material and color selections, and placement of individual architectural elements follow the principles of Vaastu Shastra, an Indian philosophy of building design and orientation that is reflected in both modern and traditional architecture, interiors, and outdoor settings.

The Global Center's learning spaces range from multifunctional classrooms, team rooms, a multipurpose event space, and informal gathering areas to personal heads-down spaces for focused learning. The center incorporates 170 guest rooms and 12 suites, a fitness center, lobby with lounge/bar, dining facility, business center, and convenience store. There is a separate administrative building, shaded surface parking, and a variety of outdoor recreational facilities and amenities.

Proposed site plan

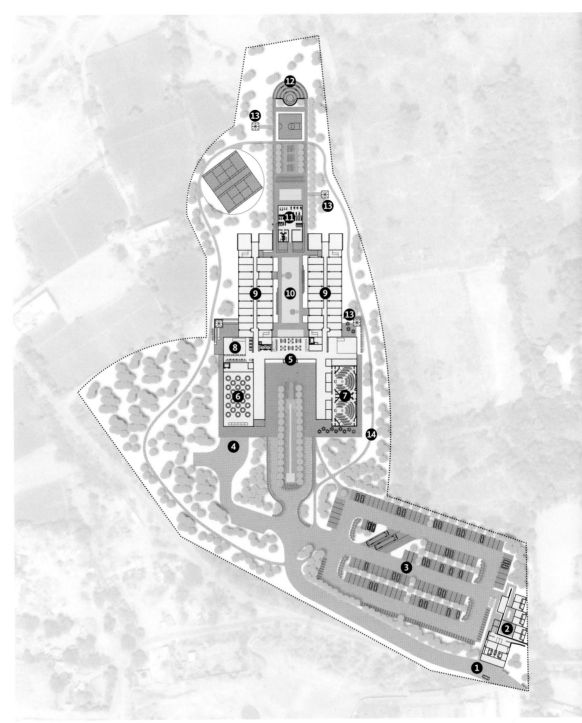

1: Main entrance gate
2: Administration
3: Parking lot
4: Garage entrance
5: Reception
6: Event hall
7: Tiered classroom
8: Dining
9: Guest room
10: Reflecting pool
11: Fitness center
12: Amphitheater
13: Gazebo
14: Walking trail with benches

0 25 50   100 ft

BELOW •• The entry courtyard, which reflects traditional Indian architecture, is a source of light and air that provides generous outdoor space appropriate for the climate. OPPOSITE •• The Global Center's porte cochere.

Arizona State University

Lattie F. Coor Hall
Tempe, Arizona, USA

In brief

Type: Classroom/office building
Completed: 2003
Size: 270,000 sf
Height: 6 stories
Green factor: Sustainably designed

One of America's largest public research universities, Arizona State University (ASU) consists of four separate campuses, all within metropolitan Phoenix. Coor Hall houses the university's social sciences programs. Named after a former ASU president, the building forms a gateway to the Tempe campus. Large lecture classes of 200 to 400 students are filmed and distributed digitally. The faculty needs offices and research labs, while students need common areas for studying and tutorials. Coor Hall separates this program vertically, with the ground plane left open as a pedestrian entry. This strategy performs well in the region's hot, arid climate, giving the building exceptional efficiency, legibility, and presence.

OPPOSITE •• The raised five-story glass box, housing faculty offices, creates a passageway that is part of a major campus entry. **OVERLEAF** •• Giving the different parts of the building their own expression heightens interest as people approach the building. Classrooms and student assembly spaces are clad in concrete.

Dr. Lattie F. Coor, ASU's president from 1990 to 2002, is credited with raising ASU's stature as a leading public research university. Coor Hall's location speaks to the desire for a signature building that serves as the gateway to ASU's Tempe campus, linking its immediate, densely developed setting to a planned expansion area to the west. Essentially an infill project, Coor Hall had to fit its 270,000-square-foot program among an existing arts center, other academic buildings, and a parking structure. With only vertical stacking as an option, the architects—Gensler and the Phoenix firm of Jones Studio—opted to divide the program, with a considerable part of the ground level left open as a campus entry.

The highest-occupancy spaces, the large lecture halls—media-intensive spaces with tiered seating and high ceilings—are placed at ground level or one story below. Easily accessed by students, the lecture halls benefit from the insulating effect of the earth's thermal mass. Their location leaves enough open space at grade to allow a major campus walkway, the "light bridge," to pass through Coor Hall's double-height entry, flanked by lecture halls and a student commons. Above them, clad in a sky-blue glass curtain wall, is the five-story rectilinear "box" that houses departmental offices and teaming spaces.

This 150,000-square-foot element complements the lecture halls below in flexibility, energy efficiency, and environmental quality. While the lecture halls' raised floors simplify upgrading of technology, the office floors balance control of solar heat gain with the provision of natural light in the interior. Clerestories bring daylight deep into the interior, while orientation and use of opaque and transparent glazing help keep the office floors cool. Rooftop photovoltaic panels also reduce the building's energy consumption. Coor Hall predates the LEED certification process, but is sustainably designed.

Green fact

Green measures: rooftop photovoltaic panel array, clerestory glazing to bring daylight into faculty office floors, variation in glazing to reduce solar heat gain, energy-efficient systems.

OPPOSITE, TOP TO BOTTOM •• Lifting the office block allows the lower-level walkway to get natural light from above. The first-floor computing center gives every student access to daylight and views. The tiered lecture halls are designed and equipped for media-intensive teaching.

Site plan

0   200   400   800 ft

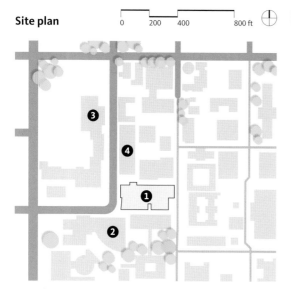

1: Lattie F. Coor Hall
2: Nelson Fine Arts Center
3: Tempe Center
4: Parking structure

BELOW ●● A tight site and sizable program necessitated that Coor Hall be a midrise building. The office box's blue exterior reflects the sky and reduces the building's apparent mass. OPPOSITE ●● Letterforms and symbols etched on the glass, the work of Chicago artist BJ Krivanek, express the importance of language as a means of communication.

Floor plans

1: Open-air plaza
2: Computer commons
3: Breezeway bridge element
4: Auditorium
5: Classrooms
6: Support
7: Main elevator
8: Main stairs
9: Offices
10: Conference rooms
11: Reception
12: Pre-school learning
13: Labs
14: Mechanical

OPPOSITE ••
a: The ground-level breezeway provides a shaded passage through the building.
b: Opaque glass mitigates the sun's heat.
c: Light slots bring daylight and air inside.
d: Thermal mass tempers heat and cold.
e: Clerestory windows help light classrooms.
f: The office block "floats" above ground level.

OVERLEAF, LEFT •• Outside the student program areas, the landings give people a place to study or socialize. **OVERLEAF, RIGHT** •• The lecture halls element of Coor Hall slips underneath the raised faculty office box.

Ground level

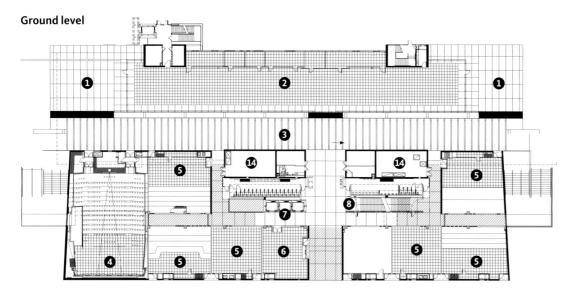

Level 2

I AM THE LIGHT OF THE WORLD

Biola University

**Crowell School of Business, Horton Hall,
Talbot School of Theology, and University Library
La Mirada, California, USA**

In brief

Type: Campus development
Completion: 1996–ongoing
Size: 15,000–98,000 sf
Height: 1–5 stories
LEED NC registered (Talbot Hall)

Biola University was formed in 1908 as an urban institution. In 1959, it moved to its present suburban campus in La Mirada, one of the gateway cities of the Los Angeles region. Biola's academic programs and student population have grown substantially over the last two decades. Since 1993, Gensler has partnered with the university as its architect and planner. The relationship has centered on developing the academic and residential buildings—including a planned arts complex and science building— to accommodate this growth. With each addition, Gensler has also sought to give the campus of this evangelical Christian university an identity and a sense of place that reflects its mission and values.

OPPOSITE •• The modern glass-and-metal curtain wall across the main façade of the library rises from a brick base that helps tie the building to the rest of the campus.

Campus master plan

1: Horton Hall
2: Biola Café
3: Hope Hall
4: Crowell School of Business
5: University Library

6: Production center
7: Talbot School of Theology (future)
8: Science building (future)
9: Center for the Arts (future)

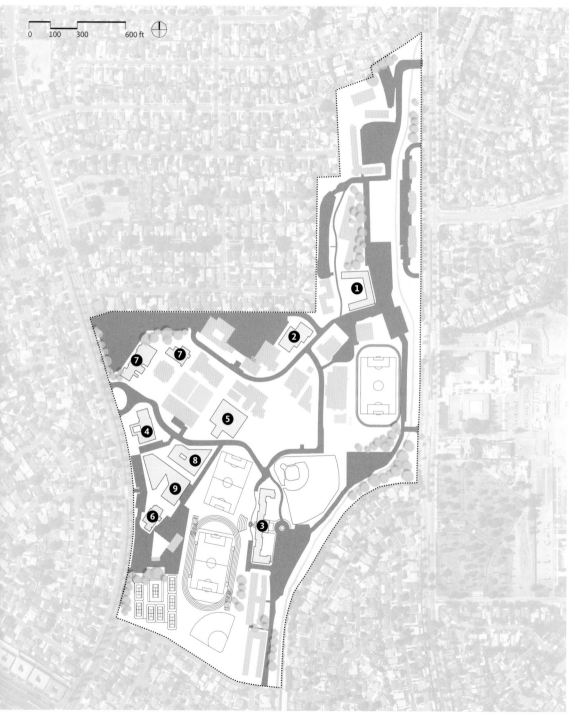

University Library

The University Library was one of Gensler's first major buildings at Biola. Designed to reinforce the prominence of the La Mirada campus quadrangle, the 97,000-square-foot library is four times larger than its predecessor. Anchoring a new quadrangle, developed at the same time, it serves as a gathering place for the campus, with a separate 120-seat reading room and a dining area with a rooftop terrace. For flexibility, the interior of the three-story building is largely free of fixed walls. The brick-clad ground floor supports two stories with glass-and-metal façades, topped with a 30-foot-high beacon. Fritted glass on these façades lets a generous amount of daylight into the building. The beacon, also a source of natural light, is lit up in the evening, making it a well-recognized landmark on the campus—one symbolic of the university's mission "to bring the light of God's truth to the world."

Horton Hall

One of two student housing projects that Gensler has completed at Biola, Horton Hall's U-shaped plan defines a landscaped courtyard as a focal point of residential life. Occupying a pivotal site between the academic core and student living, the building is clad in brick on the academic side. In the courtyard, though, plaster panels are used to give it informality. This is reinforced by the "random" placement of the five-story building's 271 windows, which gives each student's room added identity and contributes to the diversity of room types and configurations. Entered through a two-story atrium lobby, Horton Hall has 185 double-occupancy rooms, a recreation center, and a basement kitchen and laundry room.

Crowell School of Business

Crowell is a 21st-century business school. The 32,000-square-foot building opened its doors in 2007. Named for the Crowell family, a founder of the independent investment firm, Crowell, Weedon & Co., the school has a growing reputation with employers and prospective students—a prominence that the design expresses by providing supportive, technology-equipped settings for teaching and research. The two-story building steps down to one story along the west edge of the campus, giving it a scale compatible with the residential neighborhood across the street. This also brings natural light and views to the interior. Meeting rooms and tiered lecture halls, common rooms, and faculty offices are given a headquarters feeling to reflect the business world that the school's graduates will enter.

Talbot School of Theology

Talbot School of Theology is one of Biola's flagship programs, with over 1,000 students. To create a new "campus within a campus" suited to Talbot's size and prominence, Gensler has designed a two-phase redevelopment strategy. Phase one adds a 30,617-square-foot building adjacent to Feinberg Hall, the current anchor of the school's existing facilities. The new building houses classrooms; faculty offices; meeting, conference, and seminar rooms; and a chapel. Phase two replaces the existing Myers Hall with a 57,798-square-foot building with classrooms, a two-story reading room, common rooms, and a café; renovates Feinberg Hall to house a new institute; and adds a new plaza connecting the entire complex. The new buildings add channel glass and rain screens to a red-brick base that relates to older campus neighbors. Sustainable design features like roof gardens add amenity while reducing energy use.

Campus facts

Number of students	Number of programs
5,700	**145**

ABOVE •• Plaster panels and randomly spaced windows lend Horton Hall a relaxed feel.
BELOW, LEFT •• The Gensler-designed production center features a canopy-covered entry.
BELOW, RIGHT •• Horton Hall's brick-clad end façade relates it to other buildings on campus.

OPPOSITE •• With clustered seating and a second-level walkway, Horton Hall's lobby encourages people-watching and interaction.

100 - 112 EVEN
101 - 139 ODD

OPPOSITE •• On three façades, the library is clad in brick, with punched corner and bay windows for light and views. ABOVE, LEFT AND RIGHT •• The entry and lobby of Crowell School of Business are sun-protected by the roof overhang and louvers, but open and light-filled.

BELOW •• The glass-and-metal main façade and beacon make the library a campus landmark. By day, the beacon brings daylight to the interior. OVERLEAF •• The expanded Talbot School of Theology and its new plaza will be a new campus landmark.

South Texas College of Law

Fred Parks Law Library and T. Gerald Treece Courtroom
Houston, Texas, USA

In brief

Type: Law library/Courtroom
Completed: 2003
Size: 115,000 sf
Green factor: Adaptive reuse

Founded in 1923, South Texas College of Law is Houston's oldest law school and one of the largest in the United States. It occupies a multi-block campus in the city's central business district. Gensler's six-story addition to the existing college building is a technologically advanced facility that enhances the college's presence in downtown Houston. The addition and the existing building are connected at the third-floor level. To support the college's nationally recognized advocacy program, Gensler also renovated two floors of the existing building to create a mock-trial courtroom and advocacy center, with a separate reception area, dean's suite, student development center, and conference space.

OPPOSITE •• A bench for nine justices and a dramatic 20-foot wall of sapele wood anchor the two-story T. Gerald Treece Courtroom. OVERLEAF, LEFT •• Designed as a transparent cube, the new law library helps raise the college's profile downtown by displaying the activities inside. OVERLEAF, RIGHT •• French limestone expresses the strength of the college's scholastics and advocacy programs.

O'QUINN LAMINACK & PIRTLE
Hall of Champions

South Texas College of Law saw the expansion and modernization of its library as an opportunity to pull its full-block site together and give it a much stronger identity in downtown Houston. Gensler designed the building as a transparent cube, clad with a glass-and-aluminum curtain wall that provides floor-to-ceiling transparency, activating the building in relation to surrounding streets. The library's curved roof creates a recognizable profile that conceals mechanical equipment and allows for higher ceilings in the top-floor conference center. That floor is set back to make room for a roof terrace, an important outdoor gathering place for this urban college. The roof terrace replaces a courtyard that provided the site for the addition. The library provides a variety of indoor and outdoor settings for study, impromptu conversation, and larger meetings—all with wireless access. The new library is linked with the older building at the third level. To allow for future growth, the library is designed to expand vertically by up to three floors.

The college's renowned advocacy program teaches trial skills and appellate proceedings to second- and third-year students, who compete annually in more than 30 advocacy tournaments. To support the program, Gensler renovated two floors of the existing building to create the T. Gerald Treece Courtroom and Hall of Champions. The traditional appearance of the 4,000-square-foot mock-trial courtroom belies its state-of-the-art technology, largely concealed from view to put the focus on the proceedings. A 20-foot-high curved wall of sapele wood defines the judicial bench. The courtroom is reached through the 3,000-square-foot Hall of Champions, a reception area and gallery that displays the names of program donors and national championship winners. An 11,000-square-foot development center provides a variety of services, including continuing education, to students, faculty, alumni, and the Houston legal community. An advocacy director's office suite and boardroom complete the new facilities.

The George Washington University

Charles E. Smith Center
Washington, District of Columbia, USA

In brief

Type: Sports center
Completion: 2010
Size: 100,000 sf
LEED NC registered

The Charles E. Smith Center, located on the Foggy Bottom campus of The George Washington University (GW), is a significant landmark in the university's culture. It is the place where students begin their college career at orientation and celebrate at graduation; where alumni cheer for their GW Colonials athletic teams; and where fans gather to enjoy top entertainment and special events. Gensler's transformation of the 30-year-old building heightens the Charles E. Smith Center's public presence and provides new facilities and amenities for its patrons. By redesigning interior spaces, adding high-end club lounges, introducing new graphics and signage, upgrading building systems, and improving accessibility, Gensler greatly enhanced the building's performance as a campus focal point that embodies GW's energy, pride, and spirit.

OPPOSITE •• The Charles E. Smith Center lets GW compete on the court, recruit the best athletic talent, serve Colonials fans, and reach out to alumni.
OVERLEAF •• The arena's updated appearance and greatly improved seating give GW and the Colonials a sports center worthy of Division 1.

113

Each year, events at the Charles E. Smith Center draw capacity crowds. The 5,000-seat arena serves as a venue for men's and women's basketball, volleyball, and gymnastics competitions as well as campus celebrations and live performances. GW wanted to make the center easy to find for first-time visitors, and better able to handle the crush of people using it before and after events. Gensler designed a new entry along 22nd Street with a canopy, lighting, and graphics that draw people's attention and a glass façade that lets them see where they're headed. The box office is reorganized to streamline peak-time entry, while new student and VIP entrances on F and G Streets redistribute crowd flow. A new second-floor concessions concourse allows expanded food offerings and better queuing, creating a retail destination shared with temporary merchandise kiosks.

The renovated arena focuses the crowd's attention on the action. Gensler transformed the facility with improved seating; updated lighting, flooring, and finishes; and redesigned graphics and signage. The first-floor natatorium was completely rebranded with a new spectator area with expanded seating, improved sight lines, bold graphics, and new finishes and mechanical systems. To help GW recruit and retain top student athletes, Gensler designed new team locker rooms, grooming and shower areas, and meeting space; an academic center with group study areas, tutoring, and computer labs; and a sports medicine suite—twice the size of the previous one—that can treat up to 15 athletes at a time.

To strengthen GW's alumni ties, Gensler upgraded the center's club facilities. The new Colonial Club, a VIP section of the arena with courtside seating, uses high-end finishes to create a sophisticated setting for donor receptions, dinners, and events. The renovated Athletic Director's Club on the third floor provides a venue for alumni banquets, lunches, pre-game events, and ceremonies. On the lower level, a new upscale locker room gives President's Club–level alumni access to an exclusive lounge, sauna and steam rooms, individual tiled showers with changing areas, and premium wood lockers.

The Smith Center's renovation was made possible through a philanthropic matching gift from the Robert H. Smith and Charles E. Smith Family Foundations and Robert P. and Arlene R. Kogod.

OPPOSITE, TOP •• The 22nd Street entrance grabs people's attention with a new glass façade, canopy, lighting, and graphics. OPPOSITE, MIDDLE •• The Colonial Club features an amenity-filled VIP section with courtside seating. OPPOSITE, BOTTOM •• The renovated natatorium, refreshed and rebranded, includes a new spectator area with great sight lines and expanded seating.

Performance facts

Concessions sales space increase	New Colonial Club members
300%	**150**

First-floor plan

1: Fitness center
2: Academic area
3: Weight room
4: Basketball locker rooms
5: President's Club locker rooms
6: Student locker rooms
7: Natatorium
8: Sports medicine facility
9: Golf simulation room
10: Squash/racquetball

OPPOSITE, TOP •• The President's Club locker rooms raise the value of that level of membership by offering an upscale facility where members can relax and socialize. OPPOSITE, MIDDLE •• The Athletic Director's Club is a double-height volume that speaks to its prestige. OPPOSITE, BOTTOM •• The center's renovated wood-clad ticket office is a key element in a well-organized circulation plan that streamlines the flow of people during large events.

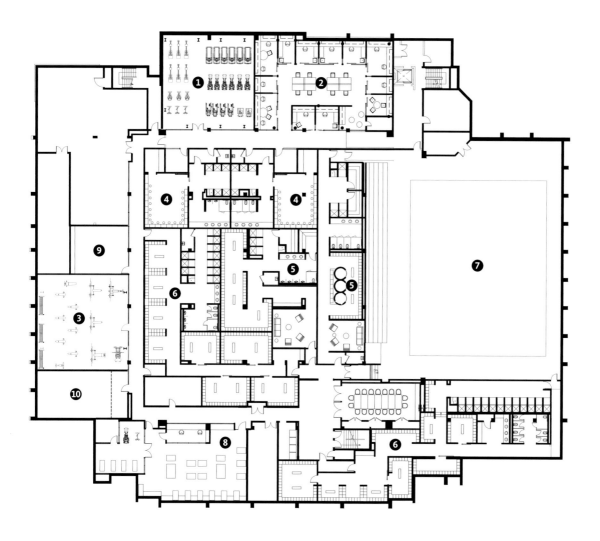

St. John's University

D'Angelo Center
Queens, New York, USA

In brief

Type: Student center/classroom building
Completed: 2009
Size: 127,000 sf
Height: 4 stories
Green factor: Sustainably designed

Founded in 1870 by the Vincentian Fathers, St. John's University relocated in 1955 from Brooklyn to its 105-acre main campus in Queens, New York. While St. John's has steadily expanded its residential programs, it still has a high percentage of commuters. Gensler designed the new 127,000-square-foot D'Angelo Center to provide a much-needed gathering place for all students. With its signature tower, the building serves as a gateway to the university and extends its academic core. With an array of facilities, including dining, the D'Angelo Center functions as the hub of campus life at St. John's.

OPPOSITE •• The tower, featuring a golden torch inspired by the Statue of Liberty, serves as a beacon for the campus and the surrounding community. **OVERLEAF ••** Located in a previously underused part of the campus, D'Angelo Center defines the edge of a new quad, with outdoor settings that encourage casual encounters.

The D'Angelo Center's location and scope grew out of a campus-wide capital projects needs analysis led by Gensler to help the university increase its diversity and expand its academic facilities to improve class scheduling and support new teaching methods. After evaluating potential sites for a new dormitory, student center, and academic building, St. John's decided to consolidate the student center and academic programs to create a gateway destination for the campus. Gensler's analysis showed that this would be more efficient to build and run, providing a critical mass of attractive and compatible uses.

The D'Angelo Center is the result—a new hub for the campus. The new building is located in an area that was underused but had excellent transit access. Gensler sited it to define the edge of a new quad. The building extends the academic core and presents a monumental façade toward the university's athletic fields. The massing and the use of fieldstone, brick, and glass on the exterior relate the D'Angelo Center architecturally to other important campus buildings. The plazas and steps along the building's main façade promote impromptu student interaction and create a safe pedestrian path along a route that was previously shared with cars and trucks.

Inside, the spacious student lounge serves as the living room of the campus—a bright, sunlit space whose towering arched windows recall the assembly hall at Ellis Island, an important symbol for a university that has served generations of New Yorkers. The first and second floors house the Center for Student Services, offices for student organizations and publications, conference and meeting space, and a recreation center. The south end of the building is for academic use, with 14 technology-equipped classrooms stacked on the three upper floors. The larger classrooms have fixed seating on tiered platforms to provide good sight lines; smaller classrooms have modular furniture that can be quickly reconfigured for small work groups or active learning activities. The full-service cafeteria on the first floor offers faculty and students a selection of international cuisines in a bright room enlivened with colorful graphics. The same kitchen supports events held in the fourth-floor ballroom, a dividable multi-purpose room seating up to 400 people, that is also used as a boardroom by the university's president and board of trustees.

Campus facts

With more than 20,000 students, St. John's has three campuses and two centers in Greater New York, Rome, and Paris. The 105-acre Queens campus is the flagship.

Design fact

Height of the center's landmark tower

144 ft

OPPOSITE, TOP •• Built on a steep hillside, the D'Angelo Center replaces old stadium seating at one of the university's athletic fields. OPPOSITE, BOTTOM •• The center's massing and fieldstone, brick, and glass cladding relate it architecturally to other important buildings on the campus. OVERLEAF, LEFT •• The double-height student lounge serves as the campus's living room, with high arched windows creating an upbeat, sunlit space. OVERLEAF, RIGHT •• As visitors enter the building, they encounter a more formal lounge with large-scale graphics depicting the university's history.

Floor plans

1: Dining
2: Kitchen
3: Game lounge
4: Print co-op
5: Student offices

6: Student organizations
7: Student publications
8: Medium classroom
9: Tiered lecture

10: Foyer
11: Central lobby
12: Open offices
13: Student services
14: Central seating

15: Concierge
16: Student government offices

First floor

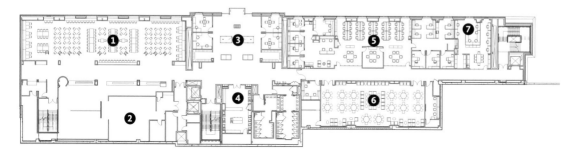

Second floor—Plaza level

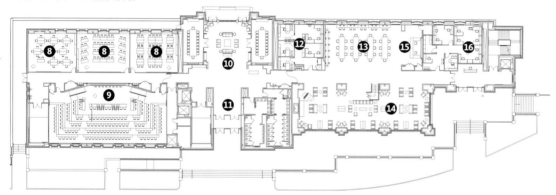

RIGHT •• The building-wide graphics program extends into the full-service dining area. OPPOSITE •• The Center for Student Services is a place where students can research opportunities for public service, an emphasis of St. John's Vincentian tradition. OVERLEAF •• The D'Angelo Center consolidates student and academic needs to create a gateway destination for the campus.

17: Medium classroom
18: Large classroom
19: Meeting room
20: Starbucks Café

21: Coffee house
22: Dining
23: Boardroom
24: Meeting room

25: Prefunction
26: Multipurpose room
27: Catering
28: Control room

Third floor

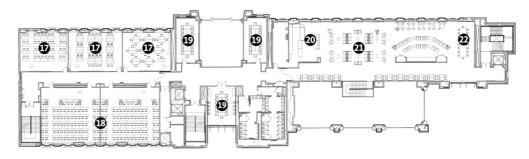

Fourth floor

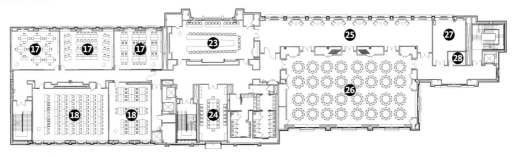

Lone Star College System

Lone Star College–Cy-Fair
Cypress, Texas, USA

In brief

Type: New campus
Completion: 2003/2011
Size: 207 acres/444,246 sf
Height: 2–3 stories
Green factor: Sustainable campus

The multi-campus Lone Star College System serves Harris and Montgomery Counties near Houston. Lone Star College–Cy-Fair, first opened in 2003, serves Cypress-Fairbanks, one of the region's largest suburban communities. The 207-acre campus is one of the few new ground-up community colleges to be developed in recent times. Designed to be the education hub of Cy-Fair, the college offers academic, career, and lifelong learning programs that serve students of all types and help support the local economy. Lone Star College–Cy-Fair is also a civic and cultural center, sharing its library, theater, and recreational facilities with the community. Gensler is now designing two new buildings on the campus.

OPPOSITE •• The campus buildings combine large window-walls with expanses of brick and concrete block. Arcades and covered walkways shelter people from rain showers and the summer sun. **OVERLEAF ••** Replanting of indigenous grasses, trees, and other vegetation restored the Katy Prairie landscape, which had been damaged by grazing.

In 2000, the residents of Cy-Fair, a suburban community north of Houston, voted to join the North Harris Montgomery Community College District (now the Lone Star College System). Gensler and landscape architects SWA Group were asked to plan and design a new college for 10,000 students on an undeveloped 207-acre site. By sharing facilities—the library/learning commons, for example, is a joint venture between the college and Harris County—the Cy-Fair campus has become the civic and cultural heart of the community.

Working collaboratively with the college's planning team, Gensler engaged the Cy-Fair community through visioning sessions, a community input charrette, surveys, and many meetings. To create a sense of place, Gensler organized the six first-phase buildings around 18 acres of lakes and retention ponds. Based on the prairie wetlands, this is a true ecosystem with fish and aquatic vegetation. It helps control flooding and treat rainwater runoff. The overgrazed former ranchland was restored as a coastal Katy Prairie with native grasses that thrive without nurturing. To avoid the heat island effect, 3,200 new trees were planted, even in the parking lots. For additional protection from sun and rain, campus buildings are connected by arcades and covered walkways. From initial programming and planning through occupancy, the campus was developed in just 30 months. New Gensler-designed student services/classroom and science buildings, phase two of campus development, are in construction.

The campus supports active, collaborative learning. Flexible studios, classrooms, and other teaching spaces are clustered so students and faculty can move easily among them. Mobile furniture makes it easy to reconfigure the spaces for small groups or large discussion circles. Workforce development is an important part of the curriculum, with an on-campus emergency services training center, technology center, advanced manufacturing center, and nursing programs that are closely linked with public, private, and nonprofit employers in the area. Wi-Fi, night and weekend access, and the range of facilities shared by the Cy-Fair community—including the conference center, library/learning commons, theater/performance venues, and fitness center—make the campus a true 24/7 setting.

Campus facts

Cy-Fair is the largest of the five LSC System campuses. Number of students:

15,175

Design fact

Size of lakes and flood control water retention ponds

18 acres

OPPOSITE ••
1: The library/learning commons offers computer stations and wireless connectivity.
2: Lone Star College–Cy-Fair shares the library with the Cy-Fair community.
3: Music programs include practice spaces large enough for an orchestra.
4: The black-box theater is an intimate and flexible performance space.

BELOW ●● Campus master plan

The campus master plan enables college facilities to double as a much-needed town center for the community. With signature spaces, landmark architectural elements, intuitive linkages among buildings, and room for future expansion, the plan emphasizes ease of access for students and residents.

1: Health science center
2: College center
3: Library/learning commons
4: Technology center
5: Center for the arts
6: Central plant
7: Student services
8: Instructional buildings
9: Science laboratory building
10: Landscaped pedestrian connector
11: Fitness center expansion
12: Food service expansion
13: Specialty building and marina
14: Loop road completion

OPPOSITE, TOP ●● Buildings and landscaping are fully integrated. A renewed eco-system of lakes and retention ponds provides a central organizing element for the campus, controlling flooding and sustaining the aquatic flora and fauna of the restored Katy Prairie. **OPPOSITE, BOTTOM** ●● Waterside pathways invite strolling, interacting, and people-watching. **OVERLEAF, LEFT** ●● A walkway from the health science center crosses the central waterway; native aquatic plants help treat rainwater runoff. **OVERLEAF, RIGHT** ●● The heath science center's atrium lobby provides places to hang out with expansive views of the campus. **PAGE 142** ●● The cyber café in the library/learning commons offers a casual space for students to meet or study.

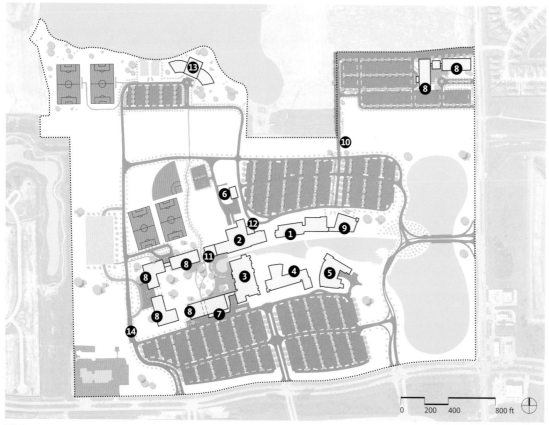

0   200   400   800 ft

Floor plans: library/learning commons

1: Lobby
2: Main circulation desk
3: Library offices
4: Library collections
5: Children's library
6: Study room
7: Cyber café
8: Information desk
9: Advising center
10: Testing
11: Assisted learning
12: Counseling center
13: Administration suite
14: Business office
15: President's office
16: Reading & writing
17: ESL program
18: Language lab
19: Classroom
20: Computer lab

First floor

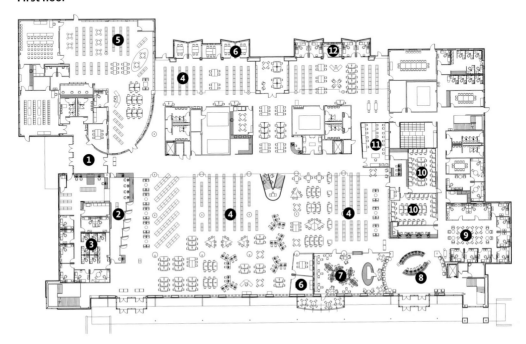

Second floor

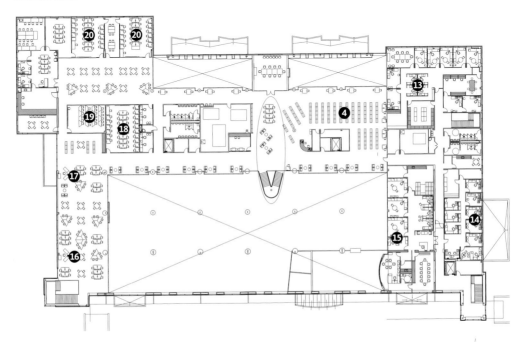

Los Angeles Community College District

**East Los Angeles College
South Gate Campus
South Gate, California, USA**

In brief

Type: Campus (new/renovated)
Completion: 2014
Size: 1.0 million sf
Height: 2 stories
Green factor: Sustainably designed

Seeking to train the regional workforce for a changing economy, the Los Angeles Community College District (LACCD) asked Gensler to help it redevelop the site of a former Firestone tire factory as the South Gate Sustainability Institute, Business Incubator, and Academic Campus. Gensler saw the 1920s-era factory building as an enclosure for mobile and fixed classrooms, labs, and workshops. The South Gate campus will allow LACCD to partner with private companies and nonprofit organizations focused on sustainability and green technologies. A major new academic and administrative building will follow as a second phase. Tangible design features like green roofs, photovoltaic panels, wind turbines, and natural lighting and ventilation will make sustainability real for South Gate's students.

OPPOSITE, TOP •• The new academic/administration building uses prominent signage as shading and to give the South Gate campus a strong presence on a high-use intersection. OPPOSITE, BOTTOM •• Among the renovated factory's sustainable features are an extensive photovoltaic array and native California landscaping. OVERLEAF •• The 31-acre campus occupies two sites diagonally across from each other along Firestone Boulevard.

The passage of bond measures for new construction and renovation led LACCD to ask Gensler's help to develop a district-wide sustainable building and renewable energy policy and an ambitious green building program, enacted in 2002, that requires all bond-funded LACCD projects to be LEED certified at minimum. The South Gate campus reflects this mandate, not least in LACCD's decision, using Gensler's analysis, to renovate rather than tear down and replace the existing Firestone tire factory building on the site. Reuse proved to be the better choice financially and environmentally. It also underscored South Gate's goal of workforce transformation by reviving an industrial remnant that had lost its reason for being.

The factory already possessed significant sustainable attributes, including clerestory windows that harvest natural light, 65-foot-high ceilings that facilitate natural ventilation, and a basement with large concrete columns that act as a heat sink. Sustainable strategies for the renovation include onsite treatment and reuse of wastewater, rainwater harvesting and storage for toilets and irrigation, a green roof and garden, and a photovoltaic array that can meet all of the campus's initial power requirements.

The renovation uses the factory's enclosed, long-span volume to introduce a mix of new elements, some mobile, modular, and prefabricated, and others set in place as landmarks to give a human scale and orientation to an otherwise huge and undefined space. The mobile elements, which resemble shipping containers on wheels, can be added incrementally, and easily reconfigured to support new activities. Also provided within the renovated factory are vocational spaces, a performing arts theater, a children's center, a gymnasium, and student activity spaces. Two smaller buildings on the site will be repurposed as office and support space for the Business Incubator.

Located across the street from the factory, near a major intersection, the new academic/administrative building is designed with an expansive green roof that provides recreational open space that South Gate will share with a nearby residential neighborhood—an area where parks and playing fields are in short supply. The building's park-like roof is planted with drought-resistant vegetation. A separate roof above the surface parking garage provides a "universal" playing field with artificial turf, suitable for a variety of sports.

BELOW •• The South Gate campus is being designed to achieve LEED Platinum. The green roof of the renovated factory supports urban agriculture as part of the sustainable curriculum. **OPPOSITE, BOTTOM** •• The nearby residential neighborhood lacks green space, so the roof of the academic/administrative building serves as both a park with drought-tolerant native plantings and an athletic field with artificial turf, reducing the need for water and maintenance.

Green fact

Renewable energy makes the former factory a zero energy building:

ZEB

Sustainable strategies

1: Internal gardens bring daylight into the building
2: Operable windows facilitate natural ventilation
3: Rooftop rainwater collection reuses storm water
4: Green roofs reduce the heat island effect
5: Clerestory windows illuminate the amphitheater
6: Thermal mass helps regulate temperature
7: Basement serves as an air-distribution system

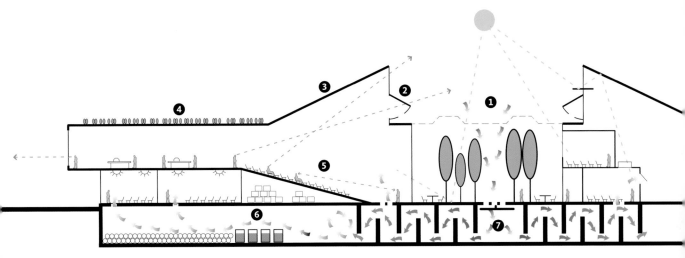

Primary and secondary schools

When old models no longer hold

Schools today are intent on creating new ways in which their facilities can support the academic and social lives of their students. Their passion for change is spurring significant design innovation.

Innovation often arises out of the recognition that the old models no longer hold—that new ideas, challenges, and opportunities need to be embraced wholeheartedly, not ignored. Such a moment has arrived for primary and secondary schools. While this doesn't in itself eliminate constraints, it does inspire passion. In talking with Gensler architects, you feel their engagement as they work with their clients to understand their intent and shape their projects accordingly. Schools are in the midst of a revolution, and Gensler's education practice is very much a part of it.

To get innovation, in Gensler's view, you have to involve everyone—administrators, teachers, and students—in the design process. While engaging on all levels "requires a lot of hand-holding," as one designer put it, it's the clearest path toward helping the school's community verbalize its needs and ideas, so that the design constantly reflects a holistic view of the school's curriculum and culture. A shared language and a common cause fuel the collaboration on which real innovation depends.

Gensler is convinced that even the tightest budgets are filled with possibility. In their experience,

constraints are a prod to innovation, not an obstacle. Take the County of Kent, southwest of London. It runs the demographic gamut from wealth to poverty. As the opening move in a countywide program of schools modernization, Gensler was asked to create a transformational design for a new school in one of Kent's hard-pressed communities, which face problems like teen pregnancy, drug addiction, and truancy. As a prototype, the design will be applied to some 150 new and renovated schools—a rollout that takes in Kent's wealthiest towns. It has to incorporate specialist facilities like a science lab and art studios. To keep the costs down, the entire program is based on a kit-of-parts approach. Yet it has to fit comfortably with the widest possible variety of site conditions and community contexts.

Confronted with these constraints, Gensler's designers focused on easing the students' transition from the disruptions of the outside world to the possibilities of the classroom inside. The school is designed as a separate, welcoming place where each student's voice is heard. An anteroom lets students remove their shoes, store their belongings, and focus. Unlike the corridors of typical schools, it is not a rigid space requiring control, but an open area of self-responsibility—more foyer than hallway. In Kent, as in other Gensler-designed schools, the building and its setting serve as a supportive helper, aiding the students and teachers rather than encroaching on them. It's the opposite of the traditional classroom, lined up off a double-loaded corridor. Gensler's learning plaza, as the prototype is called, is sustainable in a broad sense, far beyond energy efficiency, because "it allows new models of learning to happen."

Gensler's approach to Kent County's schools modernization program is an important benchmark, but it was never intended to be a universal solution. Schools are unique communities, each with its own needs and values. Consider the KIPP schools, for example. Founded as KIPP Academy in Houston, Texas, KIPP has grown to more than 80 schools across the US. KIPP also wanted a prototypical design for a school that could be replicated elsewhere, but its ethos and pedagogical is significantly different from Kent County's. As a public charter school, it has an even greater need to minimize development costs. This led Gensler to work with a different kit of parts—pre-engineered steel structures clad with corrugated metal. Inexpensive and straightforward, they're brought to life with brightly colored plaster walls. KIPP students work more intensively than most of their peers and Gensler's design gives them a supportive, hard-working learning environment that captures exactly what KIPP Schools are all about. Using off-the-shelf resources, it can be tailored to every new location without sacrificing speed or economy.

The revolution that's taking place among primary and secondary schools reflects a growing recognition that if learning fails to take place early on, society pays the price later in socio-economic terms. Mitigating the effects of schooling that never took hold is far less cost-effective than getting it right in the first place. An initiative like the UK's Building Schools for the Future (BSF) program is an example of current public, private, and philanthropic efforts to make schools true places of learning. Gensler is heavily involved in this transformation. On the ideas front, Gensler's schools practice was a finalist in Architecture for Humanity's 2009 "Open Architecture Challenge: Classroom" competition. As these case studies show, these ideas emerge from real projects designed with education clients of every type.

Well-designed schools provide a structure for learning that is flexible and open-ended, and also straightforward, cohesive, and disciplined. This is not a question of cost, but of intent: to help teachers and students do their best work. Successful schools channel the natural energy of their students by establishing a rhythm of activities that frame their days. They work with Gensler to design the settings that complement these activities—contexts for learning that can support real and rigorous creativity.

OPPOSITE ●● **St. Philip's Academy in Newark, New Jersey, uses color, natural light, communal settings, and flexible teaching environments to engage students.**

Kent County Council

**New Line Learning Academy Building Program
and County Schools Modernization
Kent County, England, UK**

In brief

Type: Schools modernization
Completion: 2008–2020
Number of schools: 130
Green factor: Up to Zero Carbon

Gensler began working with Kent County Council in 2006 on a major initiative to renew and rebuild outdated schools that is now funded by the UK's Building Schools for the Future (BSF) program. This groundbreaking effort, described by Kent County's former BSF project manager, Karl Limbert, as "a national template for how to do it," will bring modern learning environments to the county's schools at every level. From the outset, Gensler has engaged the schools, their students, and their communities in the design process. Among the resulting innovations is the learning plaza developed for the New Line Learning Academies. This agile, open-plan teaching space was first tested as a prototype and refined before it was applied to the new academies. The plaza reflects the real world that Kent's students inhabit—wireless, social, and geared to mobile work and living.

OPPOSITE •• **The learning plaza can be easily reconfigured for different activities, numbers of students, and degree of collaboration. Here, the plaza's mobile lecture seating is arranged for a single large gathering in support of project-based learning activities.**

157

OPPOSITE ●● The learning plaza prototype incorporates a variety of features that make each student feel welcome, safe, and supported. Both the space and the furniture make it easy and fast to reconfigure the space for different teaching needs and learning styles. Lighting, audiovisual technology, and WiFi make the plaza a truly 21st-century setting that is readily adapted to classes at every level, as well as to parents and community groups when they use it on nights and weekends.

Plaza prototype elements

1: Ceiling
2: Acoustic ceiling tiles
3: Biometric lighting
4: Acoustic ceiling bulkhead
5: Metal mesh
6: Projection space
7: Super graphics/ wall projection
8: Display boards
9: Breakout lecture room
10: Unisex toilets
11: Wash basins/ welcome signage
12: Entrance
13: Bench
14: AV room entrance
15: Locker storage
16: Meeting room
17: Plaza carpet pattern
18: Mobile lecture seating
19: Dedicated ICT workstations

New Line Learning Academy Plaza Prototype

Faced with a failing cohort of socially deprived students and outdated school buildings, three secondary schools in Maidstone, Kent, asked Gensler for help. Part of the solution, forged through ongoing interaction with the stakeholders—including the students themselves—was an agile, technology-rich space that could be quickly adapted to a range of learning scenarios. A temporary prototype of the learning plaza, as Gensler calls it, now occupies a renovated school gymnasium in Maidstone. While serving as a test bed for the concept, the plaza also provides modern facilities and supports new ways of learning for 90 adolescent Year 8 students.

The plaza encompasses three acoustically separate zones, plus small meeting rooms. Drawing on workplace and retail precedents, the open-plan settings use biometric lighting to help students avoid fatigue. They incorporate cinema-style projection facilities and modular, mobile lecture-style seating and office-type furniture. Everything is wireless—students have their own laptops.

Students arrive at a vestibule with personal lockers; individual, unisex toilets; and an open hand-wash area—designed to discourage bullying. They take off their shoes, a ritual that focuses young minds and helps them feel at home. The idea is to break down traditional classroom structures of passive learning. Students move at their own speed and teachers collaborate and facilitate.

"The model we are creating here will be copied around the world," says New Line Learning (NLL) Academy head Guy Hewitt. Impressive metrics back him up. NLL Academy attendance figures are 90 percent, up from 50 percent the year before. Two years on, 16 percent of students attain five A–C grades in mathematics and English, up from 3 percent; and the overall pass rate has increased, with 28 percent of students achieving five A–C grades up from 9 percent. While causality is hard to prove, it is clear that the plaza concept is freeing teachers and students to do their minds' best work. As Hewitt says, "I can't imagine a more exciting school to work in."

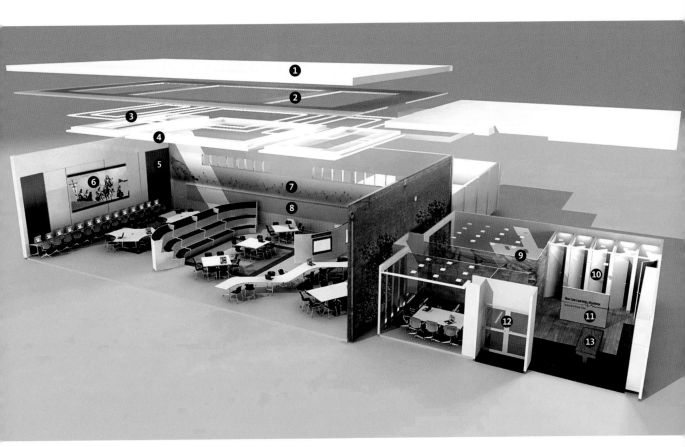

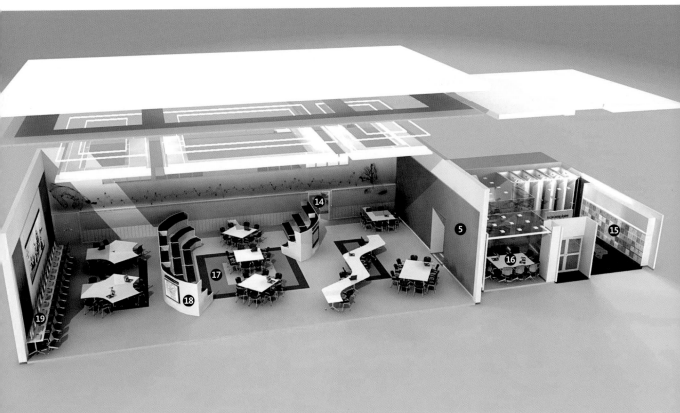

161

Performance facts

NLL Academy Maidstone rate of attendance (today)	Attendance rate of Maidstone schools replaced
90%	**50**%

NLL Academy students getting five A–C grades	Students getting five A–C grades previously
28%	**9**%

ABOVE •• Graphics and biometric lighting reinforce the academy's goals and create a calming atmosphere. PAGES 160–161, TOP •• The plaza set up during the school day for collaborative teamwork. PAGES 160–161, BOTTOM •• The same space set up with lecture-style seating for a parents' evening.

Design fact

Students per plaza, depending on year in school:

90–135

New Line Learning Academy Building Program

The plaza was developed as part of a national initiative in the UK, the New Line Learning Academy program. Gensler has designed 10 academy projects to date, either to replace existing schools or to allow two or three of them to merge into new quarters. Publicly funded, independent, and local, the academies often supplant failing schools in economically deprived communities. Backed by corporate sponsorship—Hewlett-Packard and Microsoft are involved, for example—academies offer an enlightened curriculum and state-of-the-art facilities. Their design permits community use on weekday evenings and weekends, providing a venue for meetings and adult education.

The academies' students often come from challenging circumstances. School is not always a high priority. In that context, developing emotional intelligence is as important as academic learning. The academies mix business, enterprise, and vocational studies with university-track ones, leveraging the sophisticated facilities and technology that their sponsors help make available. Along with visioning sessions with existing schools and their communities, Gensler drew on best practices in Scandinavia, China, Australia, and the US. Taking a leaf from workplace design, the students were given disposable cameras and asked to document their likes and dislikes.

Each academy has a "heart" space at the center with dining and student support space. Around this space are the different plaza zones—10 general learning plazas for Years 7–11, each for 90 or 120 students; and four Year 12 and Year 13 plazas, each for 135 students. Thanks to the general plaza's innate and supportive agility, students spend much of their time there. However, they also make use of purpose-built destination plazas for science, art, technology, and physical education.

THIS PAGE AND PAGES 166–167 •• The plaza can support several work modes at once. Its main components are the same, but the look and interior detailing can vary. **OVERLEAF** •• The new NLL Academy Maidstone features a "heart" space that links to general learning plazas on one side and destination plazas on the other.

Kent County Schools Modernization Program

Building Schools for the Future (BSF) is a $32-billion UK government program to bring county schools into the 21st century. As the schools' design advisor, Gensler enjoys a partnership with Kent County Council that predates BSF, but the program's funding is behind most of its work—a total of 52 schools designed to date. Kent's efforts follow three decades of under-investment, resulting in failing schools, "bells and cells," and growing difficulties recruiting good teaching staff. To reverse the downward trend, Kent set out to reconnect schools with their communities and give them the best possible facilities. A learning-centric curriculum is matched by the county's commitment to replace or renovate more than 130 schools over a 15-year period. Kent recognizes that learning styles and goals vary widely. It also accepts that each school has its own ethos, values, and culture—unique factors that shape its design in unpredictable ways.

Gensler used principles of mass customization to reconcile the need for scalability with the desire for tailored settings that speak to the specifics of each school—and, of course, to the site, neighborhood, and community. Instead of accepting the traditional elements of school design, like classrooms and corridors, Gensler considered the users and their activities, and how best to support them. The result is a series of spaces—like campfires (class work), watering holes (small group work), and studios (mixed work modes)—designed for diverse learning styles. For Northfleet Technology College, for example, Gensler created a "school within a school" that gives older and younger children their own realms. It is served by a "launch pad," a gathering space housing exhibits, an Internet café, and a library. Destination areas for special subjects like science and technology are given prominence in the design.

OPPOSITE •• The "launch pad" at Kent's Northfleet Technology College exhibits the type of work to which its curriculum could lead. **ABOVE** •• Kent is among the largest and most populous counties in the UK. It also has the highest secondary school population.

St. Philip's Academy

Newark, New Jersey, USA

In brief

Type: School renovation/expansion
Completed: 2007
Size: 67,000 sf
Height: 5 stories
LEED NC registered, targeting Silver

Established in 1988 by the Trinity & St. Philip's Episcopal Cathedral of Newark, St. Philip's Academy is an independent primary and middle school whose mission is to give disadvantaged inner-city children a first-rate education. Outgrowing a building that Gensler helped renovate in 1996, St. Philip's bought a 1920s-era chocolate factory building. The goal was not just to house some 320 students, but to "push us to be innovative—to be a platform for everything happening in the school," in the words of Head of School Miguel Brito. Working to a tight budget, Gensler designed the renovation/expansion "with children in mind," as famed educator Horace Mann suggested. The result is a school that is designed academically as well as socially to engage and focus its students.

OPPOSITE •• Distinctly modern in style, a new glazed vertical "lantern" above the entry contrasts with the brick façade of the renovated 1920s-era factory. It brings natural light into the building during the day and remains lit at night to act as a beacon for the neighborhood. **OVERLEAF ••** Classrooms are configured to support collaboration as well as individual and group instruction.

St. Philip's Academy

342

The education philosophy of St. Philip's Academy is "to bring a personally relevant and effective learning experience to each individual, so that the students themselves can become agents of change and improvement." The school is part of the students' social and cultural milieu, not separate from it, which explains why more than 330 alumni, many graduates of leading high schools and universities, still think of St. Philip's as their alma mater. The school is focused on healthy living—sustainability in human terms—and the building is designed to be the catalyst of that transformation.

The five-story former chocolate factory is conveniently located in downtown Newark, near universities and public transit. The site included an area at the back just big enough to add a 15,000-square-foot gymnasium and assembly hall. Large roll-up doors bring light and air into the gym. They open out to an adjoining playground, and an elevated stage between them serves events inside and outside. Previously the school lacked significant community space, so the addition is an important amenity.

The gymnasium roof created an opportunity—not for a green roof, but for a real roof garden that is an integral part of the school's active pedagogy, a way to change students' attitude about sustainability. This is an active garden that the students cultivate. Thanks to a donor, the roof now has solar panels. The roof garden takes this lesson in sustainability beyond solar energy, showing students how crops are grown, harvested, prepared as food, served, enjoyed, and recycled as nutrients for the

garden. The kitchen and cafeteria downstairs also teach students about this virtuous, natural cycle. They eat lunch by grades, sitting with peers outside their class. Round tables and an open kitchen make this a family affair. Everyone has an assigned job, with the older children teaching the younger ones.

It's also an example of the design team's determination to make multiple use of every possible space. That is reflected in the classrooms, as well. Through workshops with the teachers, Gensler developed settings that are flexible, not static. Teachers engage students, and so do the Head of School and his staff, who sit in the center of the action. The library, computer-equipped but book-focused, doubles as a meeting room that the school shares with outside groups. Beloved remnants of the old building, like a sculpted lion, are present in a building that unabashedly reveals its industrial past. St. Philip's embraces its history and relationship with the community. Continuity is a theme—the design accepts what is, then shows how it can be influenced, changed for the better.

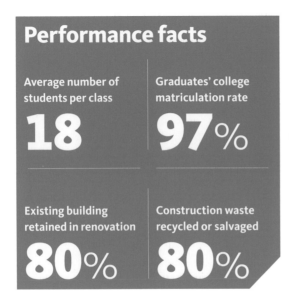

Performance facts

Average number of students per class	Graduates' college matriculation rate
18	**97**%

Existing building retained in renovation	Construction waste recycled or salvaged
80%	**80**%

OPPOSITE, TOP •• Open space is scarce in the area, so the large outdoor playground gives students a place to exercise and develop teamwork skills. **OPPOSITE, BOTTOM** •• The vegetables that students grow in the rooftop garden become part of their lunches. **OVERLEAF, LEFT** •• The garden helps students learn about sustainability and nutrition. **OVERLEAF, RIGHT** •• In the cafeteria, students sit family-style in small groups to encourage connection. **PAGES 178–179** •• The new gymnasium is also a community gathering place, with roll-up doors that allow for indoor and outdoor events.

KIPP Academy

Houston, Texas, USA

In brief

Type: Charter school
Completed: 2000–2009
Number: 4 campuses, 8 schools
Size: 27,254–69,304 sf
Green factor: Minimizes materials

Two teachers formed KIPP (Knowledge Is Power Program) Academy in inner-city Houston in 1994 as a fifth-grade public school program for students from low-income families. Today, KIPP is a national network of 82 free, open-enrollment, college-preparatory public schools, serving preschoolers through 12th graders. The founding school in Houston began as portable classroom buildings linked by covered walkways. KIPP's teachers and board members asked Gensler to design KIPP Academy, a permanent middle school in the city that would serve as a template for other KIPP schools across the country. Economy of means was a necessity, so Gensler developed a kit-of-parts solution that can be built in phases using off-the-shelf materials to provide a vibrant, highly functional environment for learning.

OPPOSITE •• **Exposed ductwork and structure elements make the architecture legible at a glance, teaching students how buildings function. Bright colors are an inexpensive way to give the interior spaces extra vibrancy.**

Per an article in the 11 July 2009 issue of The *Economist*, "A cheery yellow building in southwest Houston may not look like the center of an educational revolution, but looks can be deceptive. The KIPP schools are the most striking example of a movement that is improving education across America." The Gensler-designed middle school supports KIPP's ambitious goals with flexibility and true economy of means.

KIPP's primary goal was to provide its teachers and students with school buildings that effectively support learning and achievement—and to do so at a 40 percent lower construction cost than a conventional new public school. KIPP students spend much more time at school than most public school students do—from 7:30 a.m. until 5:00 p.m. on weekdays, every other Saturday, and for three weeks during the summer. The quality of the school experience clearly matters. KIPP also wanted the settings to stimulate student interest in architecture and construction.

Working as part of a design-build team, Gensler took a kit-of-parts approach to the KIPP school prototype, using pre-engineered steel building components to create a family of room sizes to house the school's activities and functions. To keep costs low, the buildings are clad in corrugated metal, accented and enlivened inside and out with brightly colored plaster walls. The school was built in two phases. Its classrooms, art and music rooms, library, cafeteria, gymnasium, and offices are organized around a central circulation spine. Most floors are vinyl composition tile or carpet, but the common areas use tinted and scored concrete. Duct-work and structural elements are exposed, so students can intuit how a building goes together.

The use of industrial components, including steel-framed doors and windows, reflects KIPP's pragmatic approach to education. As KIPP evaluates new locations for its schools, Gensler's kit-of-parts design approach simplifies the process of analyzing options and generating test-fit plans for potential sites. The school prototype can be rapidly modified to accommodate variations in site configuration, topography, program, and budget.

Since completing the prototype, Gensler has designed a high school and middle school on the same site, as well as several other KIPP schools elsewhere in Houston. The KIPP Sharpstown College Prep Middle School occupies a renovated office warehouse in southwest Houston. Gensler is designing the renovation of an existing office building on the site to provide classrooms, a cafeteria, and other facilities for the middle school and a new lower school. For the KIPP Polaris Academy for Boys at KIPP's Northeast campus, Gensler designed the renovation of a shopping center site to house KIPP's first single-gender lower and middle schools, along with a coeducational high school. Gensler is also planning KIPP's Sunnyside campus, which will be developed in phases as a new K–12 school.

OPPOSITE, TOP •• Playground with gymnasium in the background. **OPPOSITE, BOTTOM** •• The middle school walkway connects to the gymnasium (right). Steel-frame windows of different shapes and sizes are arranged playfully on the gym walls to soften their industrial look.

OVERLEAF •• Planar elements are used to define entries and circulation. Angled geometries and saturated colors distinguish them from the main parts of the building, which are clad in corrugated metal siding.

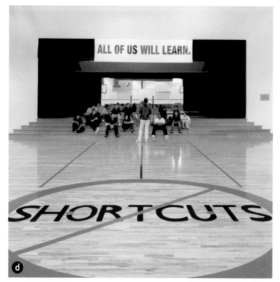

KIPP Academy relies on standardized room sizes for different functions and off-the-shelf materials arranged in specific ways to suit each school's needs.

a: Informal gathering spaces in public areas help students work collaboratively.
b: The middle school's shaded breezeway.
c: Classrooms have movable furniture that can be easily rearranged for different activities.
d: Graphics in the gym and other spaces reference KIPP's credo, "There are no shortcuts."
e: The middle school cafeteria wall is designed with encouraging mottos.
f: KIPP Houston High School is located at the center of the campus.

Campus plan
Academic buildings are clustered in the northeast corner of the campus, with athletic fields along the south and west edges, facing the densest residential areas.

1: KIPP Middle School
2: KIPP SHINE Prep lower school
3: Main building
4: KIPP Houston High School
5: Soccer field
6: Soccer/football/track
7: Kipp Hill
8: Softball/baseball field
9: Practice field

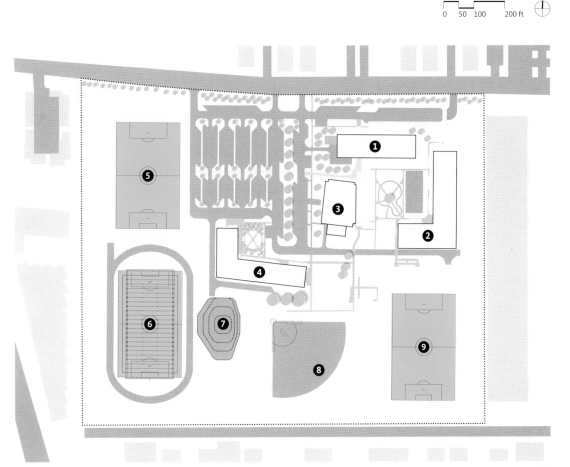

0   50 100   200 ft

Campbell Hall
Episcopal School

Community Arts Center and Campus Plan
North Hollywood, California, USA

In brief

Type: Campus expansion
Completion: 2010–2012
Size: 140,000 sf
Height: 1–2 stories
LEED registered, targeting Silver

Campbell Hall is an independent, coeducational K–12 day school. The early buildings were designed by noted midcentury modernist A. Quincy Jones. With over 1,000 students, the school recently acquired land to expand the campus to 15.5 acres. In parallel with a 2008 strategic plan, Gensler helped plan for future development, including a 95,000-square-foot arts center and a 45,000-square-foot gymnasium. As a "community of inquiry," Campbell Hall sees learning as a collaboration between students and faculty. The Gensler-designed Community Arts Center exploits the benign climate to create "interstitial" outdoor settings that promote informal interaction and tie the new and old parts of the campus together. The result is a walkable whole—denser, but with a greater sense of community.

OPPOSITE •• The Community Arts Center uses interstitial space to create an integrated, holistic learning experience that encourages multidisciplinary collaboration. **OVERLEAF ••** Upper-level gardens alternate with classrooms to create a range of common areas for interaction.

Campbell Hall's horn-shaped campus sits between the Ventura Freeway and the Tujunga Wash, a Los Angeles River tributary. The existing buildings are concentrated on the east side, along Laurel Canyon Boulevard. The first phase of the Community Arts Center redevelops the southeast corner of the campus. Built over parking for 175 cars, the 40,000-square-foot, two-story building includes classrooms and studios for music and the performing and visual arts, plus an art gallery and faculty offices. At grade, the program areas are eroded to form a pedestrian street and plaza. The built spaces and roof gardens on the upper level function as a second ground plane, with openings that overlook the outdoor settings below.

The second phase of the Arts Center is a 55,000-square-foot theater for 650 people. Most of the buildings at Campbell Hall are visible from a residential neighborhood to the east. The theater is located west of the first-phase building, to minimize the visual impact of its 75-foot-high fly tower. The built spaces on the upper level of the classroom/studio building are designed as bars, oriented east–west and separated by roof gardens, to maintain a residential scale along Laurel Canyon Boulevard.

The design of the Arts Center maps the two main conditions found at Campbell Hall: the formal, orthogonal rhythm of its original midcentury architecture, reflected in the design of the new classroom/studio building; and the informal, non-orthogonal character of campus circulation, picked up in the new pedestrian street that cuts through the building, connecting it with the east side of the campus and its main entry. Anchored by an outdoor gathering place at its north end, the street acts as an "interstitial incubator" to generate activity and increase opportunities for ambient learning and encounter. With its rooftop terraces, landings, and bridges, the new building makes Campbell Hall's diverse and talented arts community legible, accessible, and vibrantly visible.

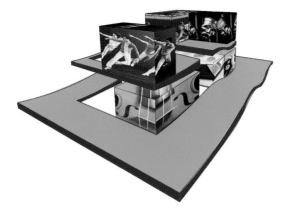

OPPOSITE, TOP •• Alternating the classroom and gardens at the upper level creates a scale consistent with housing across the street. OPPOSITE, BOTTOM •• The plaza is the heart of the Arts Center. LEFT •• Lifting the ground plane and placing classrooms and studios above and below it made room to insert a pedestrian street at grade. PAGE 195, TOP/BOTTOM •• The balcony and side boxes of the theater reference sound waves. PAGES 196–197 •• The porosity of the new center exposes the processes of art.

Site plan and ground-level floor plan

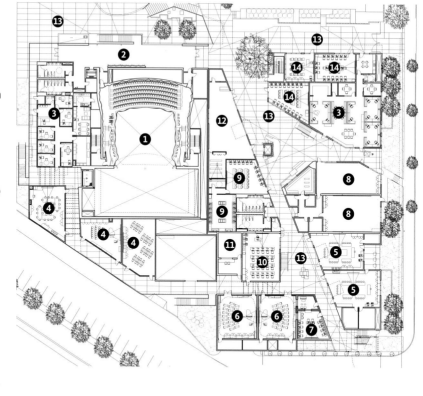

1: Theater
2: Theater lobby
3: Faculty offices
4: Elementary art/ music classroom
5: Visual arts classroom
6: Band room
7: Music recording studio
8: Dance studio
9: Photography studio
10: Video production lab
11: Video recording studio
12: Art gallery
13: Arts plaza
14: Technology- enriched classroom

Site plan and upper-level floor plan

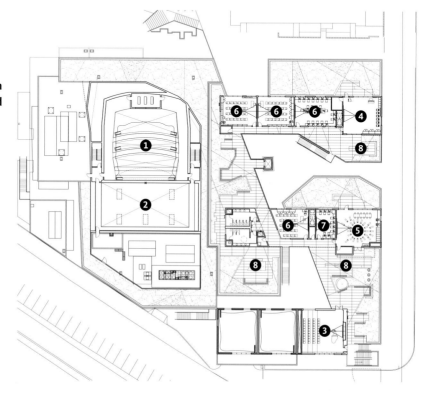

1: Theater
2: Fly tower
3: Choir room
4: Drama studio
5: Visual arts classroom
6: Technology-enriched classroom
7: Math lab
8: Arts plaza

Index

Image credits

All images are credited to Gensler unless otherwise noted.

Aker/Zvonkovic Photo: page 106; page 108; page 109; page 110; page 111, all; page 133; pages 134–135; page 136, all; page 139, both; page 140; page 141; page 142; page 180; pages 184–185; page 186, middle right

Dean Alexander: page 15; page 113; pages 114–115; page 116, middle; page 119, middle

Mark Boisclair: page i, left; page 8; page 85; pages 86–87; page 88, all; page 90, bottom; page 91; page 93, all; page 94; page 95

Benny Chan/Fotoworks: page 96; page 102; page 103, bottom

Craig Cozart: page 22, bottom

Crystal: page 116, top

Cheryl Fleming: page 11; page 48, both; page 49, both; pages 50–51

Tom Fox, SWA Group: page 20, top right; page 27, top

Rick Gardner: page 183, both; page 186, top left, top right, middle left, bottom left, and bottom right

Gensler/ASGvis: page 144, both; pages 146–147, both; page 148, both; page 150; page 151, bottom

Tim Griffith: inside front cover, right; pages 18–19; page 20, top left, middle left, and middle right; page 23; page 24; page 27, bottom; page 100, top and bottom left; page 101; page 103, top left and top right

Light CG: page 70, both; page 72; page 74, both; page 75, both; page 77; pages 78–79; page 116, bottom; page 119, top

Michelle Litvin: page ii, right; page 57, both; page 58; page 59; page 63, top left and top right; page 66, both; page 67, bottom

Michael Moran: inside front cover, left; page ii, left; page 44; page 47; page 120; pages 122–123; page 125, both; page 126; page 127; page 128, bottom; page 129, bottom; pages 130–131; page 155; page 171; pages 172–173; page 174, both; page 176; page 177; pages 178–179

Brian Pobuda: page 36

Owen Raggett/Gensler: page i, right; page 7; page 156; pages 160–161, both; page 162, all

Sherman Takata: front cover; page 4; page 17; page 20, bottom left; page 28, both; page 29, both; page 31; pages 32–33; back cover

Evan Thomas: page 60; page 63, bottom left and bottom right; pages 64–65; page 68, bottom left and bottom right; page 69; inside back cover, left

Adrian Wilson: page 53; page 54; page 55, all

The 'LEED Certification Mark' is a registered trademark owned by the U.S. Green Building Council and is used by permission.

DEMCO